11/15/90

D0915308

**Contributions of the Committee on Desert and Arid Zones
Research
of the Southwestern and Rocky Mountain Division of the
American Association for the Advancement of Science**

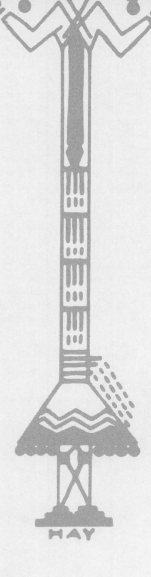

# Previous Symposia of the Series

1. *Climate and Man in the Southwest*. University of Arizona, Tucson, Arizona. Terah L. Smiley, editor. 1957
2. *Bioecology of the Arid and Semiarid Lands of the Southwest*. New Mexico Highlands University, Las Vegas, New Mexico. Lora M. Shields and J. Linton Gardner, editors. 1958
3. *Agricultural Problems in Arid and Semiarid Environments*. University of Wyoming, Laramie, Wyoming. Alan A. Bettle, editor. 1959
4. *Water Yield in Relation to Environment in the Southwestern United States*. Sul Ross College, Alpine, Texas. Barton H. Warnock and J. Linton Gardner, editors. 1960
5. *Ecology of Groundwater in the Southwestern United States*. Arizona State University, Tempe, Arizona. Joel E. Fletcher, editor. 1961
6. *Water Improvement*. American Association for the Advancement of Science, Denver, Colorado. J. A. Schufle and Joel E. Fletcher, editors. 1961
7. *Indian and Spanish-American Adjustments to Arid and Semiarid Environments*. Texas Technological College, Lubbock, Texas. Clark S. Knowlton, editor. 1964
8. *Native Plants and Animals as Resources in Arid Land of the Southwestern United States*. Arizona State College, Flagstaff, Arizona. Gordon L. Bender, editor. 1965
9. *Social Research in North American Moisture-Deficient Regions*. New Mexico State University, Las Cruces, New Mexico. John W. Bennett, editor. 1966
10. *Water Supplies for Arid Regions*. University of Arizona, Tucson, Arizona. J. Linton Gardner and Lloyd E. Myers, editors. 1967
11. *International Water Law Along the Mexican-American Border*. University of Texas at El Paso, Texas. Clark S. Knowlton, editor. 1968
12. *Future Environments of Arid Regions of the Southwest*. Colorado College, Colorado Springs, Colorado. Gordon L. Bender, editor. 1969
13. *Saline Water*. American Association for the Advancement of Science, New Mexico Highlands University, Las Vegas, New Mexico. Richard B. Mattox, editor. 1970
14. *Health Related Problems in Arid Lands*. Arizona State University, Tempe, Arizona. M. L. Riedesel, editor. 1971
15. *The High Plains: Problems in a Semiarid Environment*. Colorado State University, Fort Collins, Colorado. Donald D. MacPhail, editor. 1972
16. *Responses to the Dilemma: Environmental Quality vs. Economic Development*. Texas Tech University, Lubbock, Texas. William A. Dick-Peddie, editor. 1973
17. *The Reclamation of Disturbed Arid Lands*. American Association for the Advancement of Science, Denver, Colorado. Robert A. Wright, editor. 1978
18. *Energy Resource Recovery in Arid Lands*. Fort Lewis College, Durango, Colorado. K. D. Timmerhaus, editor. 1979
19. *Arid Land Plant Resources*. Texas Tech University, Lubbock, Texas. J. R. Goodin and D. Northington, editors. 1979
20. *Origin and Evolution of Deserts*. Las Vegas, Nevada, and Lubbock, Texas. Stephen G. Wells and Donald R. Haragan, editors. 1983
21. *Pattern and Process in Desert Ecosystems*. El Paso, Texas. W. G. Whitford, editor. 1986
22. *Small Water Impoundments in Semi-Arid Regions*. Lubbock, Texas. John L. Thames and Charles D. Ziebell, editors. 1988.
23. *Rangelands*. Logan, Utah. Bruce A. Buchanan, 1988.

# Special Biotic Relationships
in the Arid Southwest

## The Committee on Desert and Arid
## Zones Research
## of the Southwestern and Rocky Mountain Division
## of the
## American Association for the Advancement
## of Science
## Statement of Purpose

The objective of the Committee on Desert and Arid Zones Research is to encourage the study of phenomena relating to and affected by human occupation of arid and semiarid regions, primarily within the areas represented by the Southwestern and Rocky Mountain Division of the A.A.A.S. This goal involves educational and research activities, both fundamental and applied, that may further understanding and efficient use of our arid lands.

Chairman: Walter B. Whitford
Secretary: David L. Galat

Dr. Bruce Buchanan
Department of Agronomy
New Mexico State University
Las Cruces, NM 88003

Dr. Ronald Dorn
Department of Geography
Texas Tech University
Lubbock, TX 79409

Dr. David L. Galat
Department of Zoology
Arizona State University
Tempe, AZ 85287

Dr. Donald Haragan
Department of Geosciences
Texas Tech University
Lubbock, TX 79409

Dr. John Hawley
New Mexico Bureau of Mines
   and Mineral Resources
Socorro, NM 87801

Dr. Gordon V. Johnson
Department of Biology
University of New Mexico
Albuquerque, NM 87131

Dr. Wayne Lambert
Department of Geosciences
West Texas State University
Canyon, TX 79016

Dr. John L. Thames
School of Renewable Natural Resources
University of Arizona
Tucson, AZ 85721

Dr. Walter G. Whitford
Department of Biology
New Mexico State University
Las Cruces, NM 88003

Dr. John Zak
Department of Biological Sciences
Texas Tech University
Lubbock, TX 79409

Mailing Address

Dr. M. Michelle Balcomb, Executive Officer
SWARM/AAAS
Colorado Mountain College
3000 County Road 114
Glenwood Springs, CO 81601

# Special Biotic Relationships in the Arid Southwest

**Edited by**
**Justin O. Schmidt**

University of New Mexico Press
Albuquerque

Library of Congress Cataloging-in-Publication Data

Special biotic relationships in the arid Southwest /
    edited by Justin O. Schmidt—1st ed.
        p.    cm.—(Contributions of the Committee on Desert and Arid
    Zones Research of the Southwestern and Rocky Mountain Division of
    the American Association for the Advancement of Science ; 24)
        Based on a symposium held in Tucson, Ariz., in Mar. 1985, and
    sponsored by the Committee on Desert and Arid Zones Research of the
    American Association for the Advancement of Science.
        Includes bibliographies.
        ISBN 0-8263-1166-0
        1. Desert ecology—Southwest, New—Congresses.    2. Desert ecology—
    Sonoran Desert—Congresses.    3. Desert ecology—Chihuahuan Desert—
    Congresses.    I. Schmidt, Justin O., 1947–        .    II. American
    Association for the Advancement of Science. Committee on Desert and
    Arid Zones Research.    III. Series: Contribution . . . of the Committee
    on Desert and Arid Zones Research ; 24.
    QH104.5.S6S74    1989
    574.5′2652′0979—dc20                                                        89-5120
                                                                                          CIP

# Contents

# Tables

# Figures

# PREFACE

The arid Southwest, with its extreme temperature, low moisture, and high incident sunlight, abounds in biotic specializations. Many animals and plants have developed specializations that enable them to exist in this environment where their life is often so close to their tolerance limits. Adaptations to this harsh environment range from the more generalized, such as the smaller leaf sizes of most water-limited plants, to the more specific, such as the blooming of the saguaro cactus just before the end of the spring drought and near the yearly temperature peak. Still others, such as the Gila monsters and beaded lizards, are specialized evolutionary relics remaining from widespread, successful, speciose lineages that have long been extinct outside southwestern North America.

Human habitation in the arid Southwest is sparse relative to the moist temperate areas of eastern North America, yet this area abounds in a diversity of life. The Sonoran and Chihuahuan deserts, for example, are well known for possessing an enormous number of plant species (Kearney and Peebles 1960; Martin and Hutchins 1980), and there are probably more vertebrate and insect species in this area than any other part of the United States (see Lowe 1980 for a listing of vertebrates of Arizona). Nevertheless, compared to the eastern United States, few in-depth investigations in the arid Southwest of these animals and plants have been conducted. Ecological, energetic, and chemical studies are even fewer.

The Committee on Desert and Arid Zones Research (CODAZR) of the Southwestern and Rocky Mountain Division of the American Association for the Advancement of Science sponsored a symposium on desert animals and plants in March 1985 in Tucson, Arizona. The purpose of this volume, the result of that symposium, is to present detailed analyses of ways in which various biotic forms have evolved and survived in the arid Southwest. We do not intend to cover all examples, or to be encyclopedic— indeed, that would not be possible given our incomplete analyses of most species; rather, we intend to present thorough, well-investigated case studies of specific biotic relationships within the Sonoran and Chihuahuan deserts.

Large columnar cacti are the hallmark of the Sonoran Desert of Arizona and Sonora, Mexico. After an initial period of establishment, these long-lived cacti have almost no natural enemies and can withstand intense temperatures and low moisture. Storms, extreme winds, freezing, and mechanical damage typically cause their ultimate demise. Once injured or collapsed, columnar cacti serve as massive rots harboring a diversity of life forms. At this stage a combination of cactus natural products and rot microorganisms and their odors sets the stage for a most unusual set of interactions. Several species of desert *Drosophila* compete for the resources of the cactus rots. The subtleties of these competitive interactions and the chemical and biological bases that determined the evolutionary and contemporaneous outcomes of these interactions are unraveled and presented by Fogleman and Heed.

Two prominent groups of southwestern desert animals are the seed-harvesting ants and the horned lizards. The two groups have a special relationship: the ants are the primary food of the lizards, and the lizards are the primary predators of the ants. P. J. Schmidt and associates detail the general adaptations and defenses of both of these groups and then focus particular experimental attention on the evolutionary adaptations of each group relative to the other. The outcome of these specific interactions is a fascinating story in desert predator-prey relationships.

Although not considered species typically characteristic of the Southwest, termites are actually among the most crucial of all organisms in these ecosystems. In addition to being the chief decomposers of cellulose in the desert, termites are a, if not *the*, major soure of insect food for many desert predators. The importance and ecological role of termites in the northern Chihuahuan Desert is elucidated by MacKay and associates. Jones and Nutting discovered new and fascinating aspects of the foraging ecology of termites in an area of the adjacent Sonoran Desert and share their findings with us.

Abiotic stresses are well known major factors faced by all life forms in the arid Southwest. Less well appreciated are the biotic stresses (mainly competition among organisms and predation), important to the survival of desert organisms. J. O. Schmidt focuses on a particular feature, the production of spines by plants and of venoms by animals, of the organisms inhabiting the Arizona Upland Sonoran Desert and presents a case for their value primarily as defenses against vertebrate herbivores and predators. Kingsley investigates a desert-specific agriculturally engineered environment also in the Sonoran Desert. In this situation agriculture has produced a huge irrigated monoculture of pecan trees in the flood plain of the Santa Cruz River Valley. Incidental to the trees are a variety of other plant and animal species that find refuge and survival in this orchard. In a one-of-a-kind study, Kingsley describes the intertwining human social and agricultural influences in this desert area and how these forces have generated both positive and negative repercussions for wildlife in this desert agro-ecosystem.

All of the chapters in this volume concern specific examples of biotic relationships peculiar to the arid Southwest. These examples are intended to illustrate the types of fascinating specialized biological relationships that have evolved in this arid region. We hope that these case histories will stimulate further investigations and provide a better understanding of the animals and plants of the arid Southwest.

JUSTIN O. SCHMIDT
Southwestern Biological Institute
Tucson, Arizona

## REFERENCES

Kearney, T. H., Peebles, P. H. 1960. *Arizona Flora*. Berkeley, CA: University of California Press. 1085 pp.

Lowe, C. H. 1980. *The Vertebrates of Arizona*. Tucson, AZ: University of Arizona Press. 270 pp.

Martin, W. C., Hutchins, C. R. 1980. *A Flora of New Mexico*. Vol. 1 and 2. Hirschberg, Germany: J. Cramer. 2591 pp.

# 1

# COLUMNAR CACTI AND DESERT DROSOPHILA: THE CHEMISTRY OF HOST PLANT SPECIFICITY

James C. Fogleman

University of Denver
Denver, Colorado

and

William B. Heed

University of Arizona
Tucson, Arizona

## COMPONENTS AND PROCESSES OF THE MODEL SYSTEM

The population biology, ecological genetics, and evolution of any group of organisms are fruitfully investigated primarily through a multidisciplinary approach. The cactophilic *Drosophila* of the *repleta* and *nannoptera* species groups of the arid lands in North and South America are no exception. The cactus-microorganism-*Drosophila* community is considered to be a model system appropriate for studies on all levels of organization (Barker and Starmer 1982). This system is currently being scrutinized for clues to many problems in adaptation and speciation by a number of investigators.

The desert-adapted *Drosophila* species endemic to the Sonoran Desert are cactophilic saprophytes that breed in the microbial milieu of their respective host cacti. By releasing water and other fundamental nutrients chemically bound in the tissues of the host plant, the various microorganisms create a veritable oasis for adults and larvae of a variety of saprophagous insects. However, for a *Drosophila* species to successfully breed and feed in a cactus rot pocket, it must first be able to detect a suitable host cactus and second, be able to assimilate the necrotic host tissues and tolerate or otherwise detoxify antiherbivore compounds present in the plant. Chemical interactions among the cacti, the microorganisms, and the flies are, therefore, of major importance in determining the *Drosophila*-host plant relationships that exist in the Sonoran Desert.

## Cacti

The columnar cacti of Mexico are highly specialized plants, and many of them are difficult to distinguish. Recently, however, a reliable phylogeny of the tribe Pachycereeae has been constructed (Gibson and Horak 1978). The terminal members of a number of lineages of the Pachycereeae are found in the Sonoran Desert (Fig. 1.1). Our model system includes five species of columnar cacti that are placed in two subtribes within the tribe Pachycereeae. Saguaro (*Carnegiea gigantea*), cardón (*Pachycereus pringlei*), and senita (*Lophocereus schottii*) are included in the subtribe Pachycereinae, while pitaya agria (*Stenocereus gummosus*) and organ pipe (*S. thurberi*) are included in the subtribe Stenocereinae. The growth forms of these species of cacti are shown in Figure 1.2.

The two subtribes of the Pachycereeae differ in stem chemistry. An analysis of the chemical constituents of four of the cacti mentioned above is summarized in Table 1.1. The fractions labeled lipids, MeOH-H$_2$O soluble, and insoluble residue were obtained by extraction of the nonwoody tissue of fresh cactus with methanol followed by 2:1 chloroform:methanol and subsequent partition of the combined extracts between ether and water. Comparing their approximate chemical composition, variation can be seen in the first two columns, percent H$_2$O and insoluble residue. Variance in the former, however, is probably due to differences in climatic conditions and water availability in the regions where the tissue samples were collected. Although there is variability in amount, the composition of the insoluble residue fraction is similar among the four cacti and consists primarily of cellulose and other polysaccharides, lignin, inorganic compounds such as silica and calcium oxalate, and cutin from the skin of the plant. Major differences among the plants of the two subtribes reside in the lipid and methanol-water soluble fractions.

The predominant components of the lipid fraction of saguaro and senita are fatty acids esters, sterols, and alkaloids. The fatty acids esters in both species and the sterols in saguaro are not unusual for plants of this type. However, the sterols in senita are atypical because the sterol biosynthetic pathway is apparently interrupted. This results in the accumulation of intermediate forms of sterols (Campbell and Kircher 1980). Therefore, typical plant sterols such as campesterol and sitosterol are absent in senita cactus.

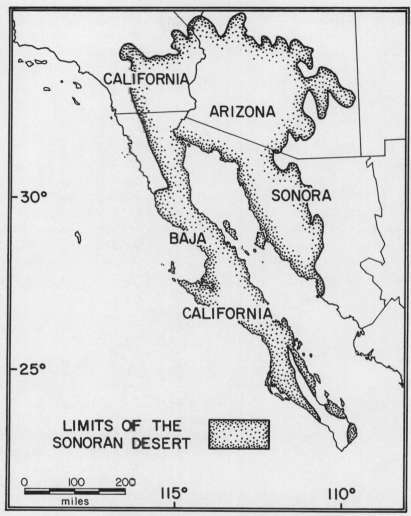

Figure 1.1.  The extent of the Sonoran Desert (from Turner and Brown 1982).

both species contain isoquinoline alkaloids. Carnegine and gigantine are present in saguaro, while lophocereine and its trimer, pilocereine, are present in senita (Djerassi et al. 1962; Brown et al. 1972). The concentration of alkaloids in saguaro (1–2% of the dry weight of the plant) is much lower than in senita (3–15% dry weight).

The lipid fractions of agria and organ pipe cacti are chemically similar and rather different from the other columnar cacti. The three main com-

Figure 1.2.   The more abundant columnar cacti of the Sonoran Desert. The common names of the species shown are *a*, saguaro; *b*, cardón; *c*, senita; *d*, agria; and e, organ pipe.

Table 1.1 Approximate composition of fresh cactus tissue (data modified from Kircher 1982)

| Cactus | Percent $H_2O$ | Insoluble Residue | Lipids | Alkaloids | MeOH-$H_2O$ Soluble | Triterpene Glycosides |
|---|---|---|---|---|---|---|
| | | | | | Percent Dry Weight | |
| Saguaro | 87 | 77 | 2.5 | 1.5 | 21 | absent |
| Senita | 81 | 71 | 6.5 | 3–15 | 25 | absent |
| Agria | 80 | 57 | 6.5 | absent | 36 | present |
| Organ pipe | 78 | 61 | 11 | absent | 28 | present |

ponents of these fractions are neutral triterpenes, sterol diols, and medium chain fatty acids (Kircher 1980; Kircher and Bird 1982). The fatty acids in both cacti are unusual in that they have predominantly $C_{10}$ and $C_{12}$ chain lengths rather than the typical $C_{16}$, $C_{18:1}$, $C_{18:2}$, and $C_{18:3}$ forms (Fogleman and Kircher 1986). Most of the triterpenes and sterol diols are mono-esterified to these fatty acids. No alkaloids are present in these species.

The methanol-water soluble fractions of agria and organ pipe cacti represent a large portion of the dry weight of these plants (up to 40%) and are composed mainly of triterpene glycosides (Kircher 1977). The methanol-water soluble fractions of saguaro and senita have not been well defined, but it is known that neither species contains triterpene glycosides. The presence of triterpene glycosides, therefore, is believed to be a subtribe characteristic of the Stenocereinae. These compounds, and the alkaloids which occur only in saguaro and senita, are a mutually exclusive pattern extending to other members of the two subtribes. This unusual stem chemistry is thought to have evolved partly as a result of various selection pressures from herbivores and pathogenic microorganisms and partly as an adaptation to survive the extremes of desert climates (Gibson 1982).

## Drosophila

The study of cactophilic *Drosophila* of the Sonoran Desert commenced with the species descriptions of three of the four endemics, *D. pachea* (Patterson and Wheeler 1942), *D. nigrospiracula* (Patterson and Wheeler 1942), and *D. mojavensis* (Patterson and Crow 1940). *Drosophila mettleri*, which is morphologically similar to *D. nigrospiracula*, was not recognized as a distinct species until much later (Heed 1977). There have been several recent reviews of the genetics, ecology, and phylogenetic relationships of these four species (Heed 1978, 1982; Heed and Mangan 1986). Life history studies were reported by Mangan (1982) and Heed and Mangan

(1986). The summary of the evolutionary histories is twofold: (1) each species appears to have independently evolved its own set of adaptations to the desert chiefly because the species are not closely related phylogenetically and inhabit different cacti, and (2) *D. pachea* and *D. mojavensis* show evidence of evolutionary origin derived from their respective ancestors south of the desert along the west coast of Mexico. By contrast, *D. nigrospiracula* and *D. mettleri* are not such clearly derived forms and are not as well known with respect to their place of origin.

## Yeasts

The yeasts that live in cactus necroses have been the subject of concentrated study for more than a decade. Of the 15 species of yeasts listed in Table 1.2, 12 may be considered as frequently encountered (>20% of the plants sampled) in one or more of the five columnar cacti. The qualitative

Table 1.2 Frequently encountered yeasts from necrotic cactus tissue[a]

|  | Cacti (Number of Samples) | | | | |
|---|---|---|---|---|---|
|  | Cardón (32) | Saguaro (34) | Senita (71) | Agria (117) | Organ pipe (56) |
| *Pichia cactophila* | + + | + + + | + | + + + | + + + |
| *Candida sonorensis* | + | + | + | + + + | + + + |
| *Pichia heedii* | + | + + + | + + + | + | + |
| *Candida ingens* | + | + + | + + | + | + + |
| *Cryptococcus cereanus* | + | + + | + + | + | + + |
| *Cryptococcus albidus* | + | + | + | + | + |
| *Pichia amethionina* var. *amethionina* | − | − | + | + + | + |
| *Pichia amethionina* var. *pachycereana* | + | + + | + | + | − |
| *Candida deserticola* | − | + | − | + | + + |
| *Pichia thermotolerans* | + + | + + | + | − | − |
| *Pichia mexicana* | + | − | − | + | + + |
| *Candida* sp. "A" | − | − | − | + + | + + |
| *Candida muscilagena* | − | − | − | + | + |
| *Pichia pseudocactophila* | + + | − | − | − | + |
| *Kluyveromyces marxianus* | − | + | − | − | + |
| *Rhodotorula minuta* var. *texensis* | − | − | + | − | + |

[a]Frequency of isolation: " + + + " (present in 50% or more of the plants sampled), " + + " (20% to 50%), " + " (rarely encountered), or " − " (absent).

data on frequency of isolation presented in this table is in general agreement with other more limited surveys in which the quantity of cells per gram of necrotic tissue has been measured (Starmer 1982a; Fogleman and Starmer 1985).

Among the 12 frequent yeasts in Table 1.2, 3 species are widespread among the cacti (found in 20% or more of the samples of at least 3 species across subtribes). They are *Pichia cactophila, Candida ingens,* and *Cryptococcus cereanus.* Four species are more common among the cacti in the subtribe Pachycereinae. They are *Pichia heedii, Pichia amethionina* var. *pachycereana, Pichia thermotolerans,* and *Pichia pseudocactophila.* Five species are more common in the cacti of the Stenocereinae. They are *Candida sonorensis, Pichia amethionina* var. *amethionina, Candida deserticola, Pichia mexicana,* and *Candida* species "A." These relationships have been thoroughly analyzed in recent years (Starmer 1981a, 1981b, 1981c; Starmer, Kircher, and Phaff 1980; Starmer et al. 1982). One of the more important concepts to emerge from these studies is the recognition of three cactus-yeast-*Drosophila* ecosystems that superimpose on the two main branches in the tribe Pachycereeae, discussed above. Two systems are found in the subtribe Pachycereinae. They are *D. pachea* breeding in senita cactus and *D. nigrospiracula* and *D. mettleri* breeding in the cardón and saguaro cacti or the moist soil beneath them. The other relationship, in the subtribe Stenocereinae, is the *D. mojavensis*-agria and organ pipe cactus system. In total, there are 4 species of *Drosophila* inhabiting 5 species of cacti in various ways and feeding in different associations on a subsample of 12 common species of yeasts.

Starmer and his colleagues have stressed the importance of the chemical differences among the cacti as factors determining the distribution and abundance of several of the species of yeasts on their host plants. The triterpene glycosides and unusual lipids of agria and organ pipe have been shown to restrict the growth of certain species of yeasts from *Stenocereus* habitats (Starmer, Kircher, and Phaff 1980). Another important factor in the distribution of yeasts is the host plant specificity of the *Drosophila.* These insects are known to vector yeasts in eastern woodlands (Gilbert 1980) and are probably responsible for the inoculation of young rots with yeasts. The distribution of yeast species, then, may be a result of a combination of factors including the *Drosophila*-host plant relationships and the chemical interactions between plants and microorganisms.

Additional information on the ecology and evolution of the cactophilic yeasts including their roles in *Drosophila* ecology may be found in the following articles: Heed et al. 1976; Phaff and Starmer 1980; Fogleman, Starmer, and Heed 1981, 1982; Holzchu and Phaff 1982; Starmer 1982b; Starmer and Phaff 1983; and Starmer and Fogleman 1986.

## Bacteria

Stems of the columnar cacti develop necrotic tissue when they become
injured or stressed. Bacteria probably initiate the rotting process although
the evidence is indirect. One can argue that bacterial action must precede
yeast growth since none of the frequently encountered cactophilic yeasts
has the enzymes necessary to break down plant cell walls (cellulase,
hemicellulase, or pectinase). On the other hand, certain bacteria do possess this ability. The observation that some rots have bacteria and no yeasts,
but never the reverse, supports this hypothesis (Starmer 1982a). Sources
of bacterial inoculum may include the soil, outer surfaces of the cacti, dust,
or insect vectors (Purcell 1982). One unpublished observation reports that
bacteria can be isolated from both the outside and inside surface of the
cactus integument even when the cactus is healthy (M. Jefferson, personal
communication). This phenomenon is not unknown since soft rot bacteria
of the genus *Erwinia* have been found within living cells of cucumber fruit
(Meneley and Stanghellini 1975).

Four preliminary surveys of the bacteria associated with decaying stems
of columnar cacti have been made in the last 20 years, but only one has
been published (Young, Vacek, and Heed 1981). The other three are in
unpublished graduate theses (Graf 1965; Vacek 1979; and Kalunta 1982). A
list of the bacterial species isolated in these surveys is presented in Table
1.3. In total, species belonging to 8 genera were isolated from saguaro and
cardón rots by Graf (1965), but most of them were unidentified. Nine genera, represented by 13 species, were found in samples of agria and organ
pipe rots by Young, Vacek, and Heed (1981). The majority of these isolates belong in the family Enterobacteriaceae. In the largest of the four
studies, Kalunta (1982) sampled 72 senita necroses and also the bacterial
flora of *D. pachea*, the resident drosophilid. Nineteen species of bacteria
belonging to 14 genera were isolated from the rots. *Klebsiella pneumoniae*
was the most commonly isolated bacterial species from both cacti and flies.
This bacterium, usually associated with inflammations of the respiratory
tract in humans and animals, has also been found in the esophageal bulb
of several species of fruit flies in the genus *Rhagoletis* (Howard, Bush, and
Breznak 1985). It has also been isolated from the heartwood and sapwood
of living redwood trees (Bagley et al. 1978). In the fourth study, spore-
forming obligate anaerobes were isolated from organ pipe and agria (Vacek
1979). Many of these isolates were identified as species of the genus *Clostridium*. Pectolytic strains of *Clostridium* species have been frequently found
in association with decay of plant material (Perombelon and Kelman 1980).

*Erwinia carnegieana* is a bacterial species characteristically associated
with necrotic saguaro tissue (Lightle, Standring, and Brown 1942; Boyle

Table 1.3. Bacterial isolates from necrotic cactus tissue

| | Cacti[a] | | | |
|---|---|---|---|---|
| | Saguaro | Senita | Agria | Organ Pipe |
| Aeromonas hydrophila | − | + | − | − |
| Acromobacter sp. | − | + | − | − |
| Alcaligenes sp. | − | + | − | − |
| Bacillus laterosporus | + | + | − | + |
| Bacillus sp. | − | + | − | − |
| Citrobacter freundii | − | + | − | − |
| Citrobacter sp. | − | + | + | + |
| Clostridium sp. | na | na | + | + |
| Enterobacter aerogenes | + | + | − | + |
| Enterobacter agglomerans | − | − | + | − |
| Enterobacter cloacae | + | + | + | − |
| Erwinia carnegieana | + | + | + | + |
| Escherichia coli | − | + | + | + |
| Hafnia alvei | − | + | − | − |
| Klebsiella ozaenae | + | − | + | − |
| Klebsiella pneumoniae | − | + | − | + |
| Leuconostoc sp. | − | − | + | + |
| Micrococcus denitrificans | − | + | − | − |
| Pseudomonas denitrificans | − | + | − | − |
| Pseudomonas fluorescens | − | + | − | − |
| Staphylococcus saprophyticus | − | + | − | − |
| Staphylococcus sp. | + | − | − | + |
| Xanthomonas sp. | − | + | − | − |
| Yersinia enterocolitica | − | − | + | − |

[a]na = not assayed

1949; Alcorn and May 1962). This species can be isolated from rots in other species of columnar cacti as well (Table 1.3). Species of *Erwinia* are known to produce soft rot in a variety of plants, especially fleshy vegetables (Graham 1964; Perombelon and Kelman 1980). Although the early work on *E. carnegieana* referred to it as a causal agent in cactus disease, this bacterium does not appear to be a phytopathogen in cacti since extensive rot formation does not typically occur when healthy plants or even slightly injured plants are injected with the bacterium (Steenbergh 1970).

In summary, these studies are interesting because of the role that bacteria play in *Drosophila* nutrition (Begon 1982 and references therein). For

example, one Australian study reported that bacteria alone were equal to
or better than any of 8 cactophilic yeast species with respect to nutritional
sufficiency for *D. buzzatii* (Vacek 1982). The surveys of cactus bacteria also
show that the diversity of genera in necrotic cactus tissue is high compared with the cactophilic yeasts which are represented by only 4 or 5
common genera (Starmer et al. 1982). However, except for the work on
senita, sample sizes for these preliminary surveys are very small, and direct
quantification of the bacterial species in any cactus has yet to be accomplished. Quantification in senita was inferred from counts of colony morphs
which can be misleading.

## DROSOPHILA-HOST PLANT RELATIONSHIPS

Extensive collections over the past 25 years have firmly established the
*Drosophila*-host plant relationships (Table 1.4). The Sonoran Desert can
be divided into two separate regions: the Baja California Peninsula and
the mainland. The climatic differences between the two areas are accom-
panied by vegetational differences, which include the columnar cacti. The
geographic distributions of saguaro and cardón are almost mutually exclusive with a small region of overlap on the coast of Sonora, Mexico, north
and south of Kino Bay. Necrotic stems of these two cacti are used by *D.
nigrospiracula*, while *D. mettleri* breeds in soils which have been inundated with rot juice from either cactus. The ability to utilize soaked soils
as larval substrates makes *D. mettleri* virtually unique among members of
the genus. *Drosophila mojavensis* uses agria rots on the Baja California
Peninsula and organ pipe rots on the mainland. Agria is essentially lim-

Table 1.4. Relative abundance of the major substrates (host plants) of the
four endemic species of *Drosophila* in the Sonoran Desert (from Heed 1978)

| Substrate | Abundance on Peninsula | Abundance on Mainland | Resident *Drosophila* Species |
|---|---|---|---|
| Saguaro | absent | + + + | *D. nigrospiracula* |
| Cardón | + + +[a] | +[b] | *D. nigrospiracula* |
| Saguaro soil | absent | + + + | *D. mettleri* |
| Cardón soil | + + + | + | *D. mettleri* |
| Senita | + + + | + + + | *D. pachea* |
| Agria | + + + | + | *D. mojavensis* |
| Organ pipe | + + + | + + + | *D. mojavensis* |

[a]Relatively common or abundant
[b]Rare

ited to the peninsula except for the coastal region mentioned above. Although organ pipe is distributed over both the peninsula and the mainland, it is virtually ignored as a substrate by *D. mojavensis* if agria is present. Due to the differences in geographic distribution of the cacti (and the preference of *D. mojavensis* for agria), three of the four endemic *Drosophila* species shift host plants (or substrates) between Baja and the mainland. Senita cactus is abundant in both areas, and *D. pachea*, which uses it as a substrate, is the only species which does not exhibit a host plant shift.

Indications of host plant specificity of the cactophilic *Drosophila* have been reported by Fellows and Heed (1972) and, more recently, by Heed and Mangan (1986). Rearing records, obtained by collecting necrotic cactus stems and allowing the flies to eclose in laboratory containers, and records of the adults collected directly from natural substrates provide a wealth of information on this subject. Although host plant specificity is not absolute, it is very high in certain parts of the desert and in certain times of the year. In general, specificity of the relationships presented in Table 1.4 exceeds 95%. That is, 95% (or more) of the flies caught on or reared out of a rot on a particular species of cactus are the resident *Drosophila* species for that cactus. Rosenzweig (1979) predicted that more sharply differentiated habitat selection should occur in regions of greater stability or in which there is only a single variable that controls carrying capacities common to all species. The stress region in Baja California, as defined by Heed (1978), agrees with this description, and it is the area in the Sonoran Desert where host plant selection is the highest.

Insect-host plant relationships, in a general sense, comprise two separate phenomena: host plant selection and host plant utilization. The former may be defined as the behavioral preference for a particular host plant while the latter represents the ability of an insect to use the plant as a substrate. Host plant selection can be based on chemical cues which inform the insect of the location of suitable plants. Chemical factors involved in host plant utilization include tolerance to toxic phytochemicals and strict requirements for nutritional factors which may not occur in all potential host plants. The remainder of this chapter will deal with the chemistry of host plant utilization and host plant selection in the cactus-microorganism-*Drosophila* model system. Parts of this subject have recently been reviewed by Heed and Mangan (1986).

## HOST PLANT UTILIZATION

Despite the fact that the endemic *Drosophila* exhibit high degrees of behavioral specificity for host plants, factors involved in host plant utilization are still important since they reflect the set of selection pressures which currently act to maintain the specificities or which historically acted to produce them. Given the five cactus species plus soaked soils and four species of *Drosophila,* there are 24 possible substrate-fly combinations (Table 1.5). Six of these combinations represent the normal *Drosophila*-host plant relationships, leaving 18 combinations which do not typically occur in nature. Eight of these 18 exclusions, or approximately 44%, are primarily due to chemistry. Chemistry may also be important in inhibiting *D. pachea, D. mojavensis,* and *D. nigrospiracula* from utilizing soaked soils, but the appropriate tests have not been performed. The biological and chemical factors involved in host plant utilization by the desert *Drosophila* are summarized in the table. These will be discussed on a case-by-case basis.

## Senita Cactus and *D. pachea*

Phytosterols in senita cactus have now been firmly established as the primary determinant of the host plant specificity of *D. pachea* (Fogleman, Duperret, and Kircher 1986). The *D. pachea*–senita story began in the mid-1960s with the observation that this fly species bred only in necrotic stems of senita and could not be reared from standard *Drosophila* media unless a cube of senita were added (Heed and Kircher 1965). As has been previously mentioned, the later steps in the pathways to typical phytosterols are either absent or inhibited, and eight intermediate forms (for example, 4α-methyl, $\Delta^7$-, and $\Delta^{8,14}$-sterols) have been identified (Campbell and Kircher 1980). *Drosophila pachea* has evolved a dependency on two of these sterols to the extent that the more typical plant sterols, campesterol and sitosterol, and the yeast sterol, ergosterol, are not adequate for female fertility or larval viability (Heed and Kircher 1965; Goodnight and Kircher 1971). *Drosophila,* like all other investigated insects, need dietary sterols since they cannot synthesize them *de novo.* The biological function of sterols in *Drosophila* includes incorporation into membranes and the sterols' role as precursors for steroid hormones, for example, ecydsone (Kircher 1982b). The two sterols in senita that fulfill the unique sterol requirement of *D. pachea* (7-cholestenol and 7-campestenol) are not found in any of the other columnar cacti in the model system. *Drosophila pachea,* therefore, is limited to a monophagous existence and cannot use agria, organ pipe, saguaro, or cardón because they are nutritionally deficient.

The senita alkaloids, lophocereine and its trimer pilocereine, have been shown to be toxic to eight species of *Drosophila* which typically or periodically inhabit the Sonoran Desert (Kircher et al. 1967). Included among these eight species were *D. nigrospiracula* and *D. mojavensis.* In tests of the effect of senita alkaloids on egg-to-adult viability and adult longevity,

Table 1.5. Biological and chemical factors involved in host plant utilization by cactophilic *Drosophila*

| | Agria | Organ Pipe | Saguaro | Cardón | Senita | Soils |
|---|---|---|---|---|---|---|
| *D. pachea* | nutritionally deficient (lack required sterols) | | | | normal host | physical and/or chemical |
| *D. mojavensis* | normal host | normal host | interspecific competition | | intolerance to alkaloids | physical and/or chemical |
| *D. nigrospiracula* | intolerance to fatty acids and sterol diols | | normal host | normal host | intolerance to alkaloids | physical and/or chemical |
| *D. mettleri* | behavior | | | | | normal host |

*D. pachea* and *D. mettleri* were the only species that could tolerate these compounds (Fogleman, Heed, and Kircher 1982). The presence of toxic alkaloids in senita excludes other species (except *D. mettleri)* from feeding and breeding in necrotic stems of this plant. Although *D. mettleri* utilizes senita as a feeding site, it prefers to oviposit on soaked soils and has never been reared from senita rots.

## Agria and Organ Pipe Cacti and *D. mojavensis*

Both of these cacti are used by *D. mojavensis* as breeding substrates. The question here is what prevents *D. nigrospiracula* and *D. mettleri* from utilizing them? Extensive field and laboratory studies have demonstrated that *D. nigrospiracula* larvae have greatly reduced viability in these substrates. For example, the combined progeny production of *D. nigrospiracula* females on agria and organ pipe was less than 14% of their combined production on saguaro and cardón (Fellows and Heed 1972).

In order to determine which chemical constituents of agria and organ pipe were responsible for the reduced viability of *D. nigrospiracula,* various chemical fractions of organ pipe tissue (recall that agria is chemically similar) were added to saguaro homogenate, and the average percent viabilities of *D. mojavensis* and *D. nigrospiracula* larvae were measured (Fogleman, Duperret, and Kircher 1986). Ecologically realistic concentrations of each fraction were employed. The chemical constituents of organ pipe which had no significant effect on larval viability include triterpene glycosides, triterpene acids (aglycones from triterpene glycosides), crude lipids, and the two major neutral triterpenes, betulin and calenduladiol. Free sterol diols, however, had a highly significant effect on *D. nigrospiracula* larvae and free fatty acids significantly reduced the larval viability of both species, but their effect on *D. nigrospiracula* was noticeably greater. A subsequent study on fatty acids, which considered the relative composition of the fatty acid fractions of agria and organ pipe with respect to chain length and viability effects, indicated that capric acid ($C_{10}$) is the most biologically important fatty acid in this model system (Fogleman and Kircher 1986). Most of the fatty acids and sterol diols in fresh tissue of agria and organ pipe are esterified to each other. When complexed in this fashion, they are apparently not toxic since the addition of crude lipids to saguaro homogenate at concentrations up to 10% dry weight had no significant effect on viability. Free fatty acids, as well as sterol diols and triterpenes, are released during the rotting process by microbial hydrolysis (Fogleman, Duperret, and Kircher 1986). The greater tolerance of *D. mojavensis* to medium-chain fatty acids and the intolerance of *D. nigrospiracula* to both fatty acids and sterol diols support the statement that both compounds are involved in the exclusion of *D. nigrospiracula* from agria and organ pipe substrates.

Laboratory experiments have demonstrated that the viability of *D. mettleri* on organ pipe is equal to that of *D. mojavensis*, and, although its viability is somewhat reduced, *D. mettleri* can also utilize agria (Fogleman 1984). Again, *D. mettleri*'s strong preference for soil breeding explains its absence.

## Soaked Soil Substrates and *D. mettleri*

*Drosophila mettleri* appears to be opportunistic in its substrate utilization. In addition to soils soaked by cardón and saguaro rot juice, it has been reared from naturally occurring organ pipe–soaked soil (Fogleman, Hackbarth, and Heed 1981) and artificially produced senita-soaked soil (Fogleman, Heed, and Kircher 1982). It is likely that soils soaked by agria rot juice are used as well, but no rearing records have been obtained on this substrate. Soils inundated with organ pipe, agria, or senita rot juice cannot be as abundant as the cardón-saguaro type because of the smaller physical size of these cacti and the relative rarity of sufficiently extensive rots for soaking the soil. Thus, *D. mettleri* may be essentially limited to saguaro and cardón due to substrate availability.

This species of cactophilic fly shares its normal substrate with *D. nigrospiracula* but only with respect to adult feeding site. There is a virtually complete niche separation between these two species for breeding site—*D. nigrospiracula* in necrotic tissue and *D. mettleri* in soaked soil. Viability studies have demonstrated that *D. nigrospiracula* larvae cannot utilize saguaro-soaked soil (Fogleman, Hackbarth, and Heed 1981). This inability is probably not due to nutritional deficiency of the substrate, at least with respect to yeast density (Fogelman and Heed 1981). A recent study suggested that, in general, soaked soils are substrates where the secondary plant compounds produced by the cacti become more concentrated due to the evaporation of water. Meyer and Fogleman (1987) have found that concentrations of alkaloids in saguaro-soaked soils measured from 1.6 to 30 times the average concentration in fresh saguaro tissue. They also showed that the viability of *D. nigrospiracula* larvae was reduced to near zero at a saguaro alkaloid concentration of 5 times that of fresh tissue. It should be pointed out that, like *D. nigrospiracula*, *D. pachea* larvae are not viable in senita-soaked soils and *D. mojavensis* are not viable in agria- and organ pipe–soaked soils (Fogleman 1984). The possibility remains, however, that soaked soils have a physical effect on larval viability as well as higher concentrations of phytochemicals.

Another question which remains concerns the restriction of *D. mettleri* to soil substrates in nature when laboratory experiments indicate that the larvae survive as well in necrotic cactus tissues as in the soil. There is little evidence that *D. nigrospiracula* drastically affects the fitness of *D. mettleri* in laboratory competition tests (Mangan 1982; Heed and Mangan 1986). On freshly rotted saguaro, *D. mettleri* slows larval development somewhat in the face of increasing densities of *D. nigrospiracula*. However, on rotting saguaro that has been aged for 14 days, emerging *D. mettleri* adults actually gain in thorax size with increasing densities of *D. nigrospiracula*. One is left with the possibility that *D. mettleri* has other competitors, such as species of the dipteran Neriidae and Syrphidae, that are usually associated with older fermenting saguaro tissue (Heed and Mangan 1986).

## Saguaro and Cardón and *D. nigrospiracula*

Saguaro and cardón are considered to be the least chemically complex of all the columnar cacti (Kircher 1982a). Both species are known to contain isoquinoline alkaloids but their concentrations are not sufficient to be toxic to larvae of any of the cactophilic *Drosophila*. The nutritional exclusion of *D. pachea* and the behavioral preference of *D. mettleri* with respect to saguaro and cardón have already been discussed. *Drosophila mojavensis*, however, have been both aspirated and reared from natural saguaro rots in low frequency. Laboratory tests indicate that the productivity of *D. mojavensis* on saguaro or cardón is equal to its productivity on agria and significantly greater than on organ pipe (Fellows and Heed 1972). Saguaro tissue, however, appears to have a detrimental effect on adult longevity (Brazner, Aberdeen, and Starmer 1984). Also, several studies suggest that the interaction between *D. nigrospiracula* and *D. mojavensis* may be a combination of larval competition and behavioral inhibition of oviposition (Fellows and Heed 1972; Mangan 1982; Heed and Mangan 1986). Rosenzweig (1979) theoretically analyzed this case in which habitat choice of *D. mojavensis* depends upon the relative densities of the two species. At low densities of *D. nigrospiracula* and high effective densities of *D. mojavensis*, the latter species should prefer to use saguaro (or cardón). A change in the relative densities would force *D. mojavensis* to use organ pipe (or agria) and abandon saguaro (or cardón). Habitat selection of this type would eliminate the negative effects of interspecific competition. The field data on the utilization of saguaro by *D. mojavensis* appear to follow this pattern (Heed and Mangan 1986).

## HOST PLANT SELECTION

The realization that certain volatiles are generally attractive to drsophilids dates from the turn of the century (Barrows 1907). Volatiles known to be attractive to *Drosophila melanogaster* include ethanol, ethyl acetate, amyl alcohol, acetic and lactic acids, acetaldehyde, diacetyl, acetoin, and indole (Barrows 1907; Hutner, Kaplan, and Enzmann 1937). Mixtures of attractive volatiles are usually much more attractive than single compounds. Other generalizations which are supported in the literature are that smaller flies and males are less responsive to odors than larger flies and females; there is a range of concentrations that elicits adult attraction above which the volatile of repellent (Reed 1938) and different *Drosophila* species respond differently (West 1961).

There is little doubt that *Drosophila* locate feeding and breeding substrates by positive chemotaxis toward fermentation by-products. The olfactory sense organs which are responsible for this directed movement are located in the third or terminal segment of the antennae (Barrows 1907). Begg and Hogben (1946) demonstrated that antennaless phenotypes of *D. melanogaster* do not respond to atractive chemical stimuli. Close range substrate location is accomplished by orientation adjustment for unequal stimulation of the antennae since removal of one antenna results in circular fly movement when exposed to food odors (Barrows 1907).

## Differences in Cactus Volatile Patterns

The hypothesis that volatiles are the chemical basis of substrate selection in the Sonoran Desert rests on the demonstration that the volatile patterns produced in the necroses of different cactus species are, in fact, different (Fogleman 1982). Table 1.6 presents data on the concentrations of the predominant volatiles found in naturally occurring *Drosophila* substrates. Methods for determining the concentrations of volatiles are presented in Starmer et al. (1986). One-way analysis of variance tests were performed on all volatiles that occurred in three or more of the substrates, and the results of these tests are also given in Table 1.6. The difficulty in pointing out significant differences in the volatile patterns between cactus species is twofold. First, volatile patterns change over time (Vacek 1979). The stages of rotting which are most attractive to *Drosophila* are not necessarily the stages that were sampled. The data in this table come from a wide variety of rot stages, yet some evidence suggests that *Drosophila* are most attracted to the initial or early stages of the rotting process (Starmer 1982a). Second, individual volatiles may not be as important as the pattern of combinations of volatiles. Nevertheless, some general differences in these data are worthy of acknowledgment. Organ pipe and agria are different from saguaro and senita in that they contain higher concentrations of ethanol. Agria also has greater concentrations of lower molecular weight volatiles (such as acetone, 1-propanol, 2-propanol, and the propyl

Table 1.6. Concentrations of volatiles in *Drosophila* substrates (in mM). Results of one-way analysis of variance tests are also given

| | Subtribe Stenocereinae | | | | Subtribe Pachycereinae | | | | | | |
| | Agria (N = 7) | | Organ Pipe (N = 36) | | Saguaro (N = 18) | | Saguaro Soil (N = 18) | | Senita (N = 8) | | F |
| | Avg ± SD | Max | Avg ± SD | Max | Avg ± SD | Max | Avg ± SD | Max | Avg ± SD | Max | |
|---|---|---|---|---|---|---|---|---|---|---|---|
| Ethanal | 0.1 ± 0.1 | 0.4 | 0.0 ± 0.1 | 0.9 | 0.0 ± 0.0 | 0.1 | 0.0 ± 0.0 | 0.1 | 0.0 ± 0.0 | 0.1 | — |
| Methanol | 9.6 ± 8.3 | 33.1 | 3.6 ± 5.9 | 30.6 | 6.7 ± 5.7 | 20.9 | 7.9 ± 8.2 | 24.9 | 6.0 ± 8.1 | 22.9 | 1.84 |
| Acetone | 2.2 ± 3.5 | 9.5 | 0.1 ± 0.1 | 0.3 | 0.0 ± 0.1 | 0.1 | 0.0 ± 0.0 | 0.1 | 0.1 ± 0.1 | 0.3 | 8.37[c] |
| Methyl Acetate | 0.0 ± 0.1 | 0.1 | 0.1 ± 0.1 | 0.3 | 0.1 ± 0.1 | 0.2 | 0.1 ± 0.1 | 0.2 | 0.0 ± 0.0 | 0.0 | 2.09 |
| Ethanol | 5.0 ± 9.4 | 25.1 | 3.7 ± 13.9 | 81.5 | 0.5 ± 1.1 | 4.9 | 0.3 ± 0.3 | 0.9 | 0.5 ± 0.4 | 1.1 | 0.57 |
| 2-Propanol | 15.9 ± 27.8 | 75.4 | 0.1 ± 0.3 | 1.2 | 0.2 ± 0.5 | 1.7 | 0.3 ± 0.9 | 2.3 | 0.8 ± 1.3 | 3.5 | 5.96[c] |
| Ethyl Acetate | 0.0 ± 0.0 | 0.2 | 0.0 ± 0.0 | 0.2 | 0.0 ± 0.0 | 0.0 | 0.0 ± 0.0 | 0.0 | 0.0 ± 0.0 | 0.0 | — |
| 1-Propanol | 3.2 ± 4.2 | 11.9 | 0.6 ± 1.2 | 6.4 | 0.3 ± 0.6 | 2.3 | 0.3 ± 0.5 | 1.3 | 1.5 ± 2.0 | 5.5 | 4.80[b] |
| 2-Propyl Acetate | 1.2 ± 2.3 | 5.6 | 0.0 ± 0.1 | 0.6 | 0.1 ± 0.2 | 0.6 | 0.0 ± 0.0 | 0.0 | 0.1 ± 0.1 | 0.4 | 7.41[c] |
| 1-Propyl Acetate | 0.0 ± 0.0 | 0.1 | 0.0 ± 0.0 | 0.2 | 0.0 ± 0.0 | 0.0 | 0.0 ± 0.0 | 0.0 | 0.0 ± 0.0 | 0.1 | — |
| 1-Butanol | 0.1 ± 0.1 | 0.2 | 0.0 ± 0.0 | 0.3 | 0.0 ± 0.0 | 0.1 | 0.0 ± 0.0 | 0.1 | 0.0 ± 0.1 | 0.1 | 0.92 |
| Acetoin | 0.2 ± 0.6 | 2.1 | 0.9 ± 1.9 | 7.6 | 0.5 ± 1.0 | 4.2 | 1.2 ± 1.8 | 5.1 | 0.1 ± 0.1 | 0.3 | 3.30[a] |
| Acetic Acid | 35.4 ± 23.7 | 82.1 | 10.5 ± 9.2 | 39.3 | 19.6 ± 28.0 | 115.4 | 23.4 ± 24.3 | 75.7 | 31.8 ± 34.9 | 98.6 | — |
| 1-Pentanol | 0.0 ± 0.0 | 0.2 | 0.0 ± 0.0 | 0.2 | 0.0 ± 0.0 | 0.0 | 0.0 ± 0.0 | 0.0 | 0.0 ± 0.0 | 0.0 | — |
| Propionic Acid | 14.9 ± 11.8 | 39.6 | 7.3 ± 9.5 | 44.7 | 3.8 ± 10.4 | 44.5 | 5.4 ± 6.8 | 17.8 | 5.9 ± 5.4 | 14.6 | 1.83 |
| 2,3-Butanediol | 4.1 ± 5.4 | 18.3 | 4.0 ± 9.9 | 43.6 | 3.2 ± 6.2 | 23.9 | 4.0 ± 5.2 | 13.0 | 3.6 ± 7.0 | 20.3 | 0.03 |
| iso-Butyric Acid | 0.1 ± 0.2 | 0.6 | 0.0 ± 0.1 | 0.7 | 0.0 ± 0.2 | 0.7 | 0.1 ± 0.1 | 0.3 | 0.0 ± 0.0 | 0.0 | 1.78 |
| n-Butyric Acid | 3.2 ± 2.6 | 8.8 | 0.6 ± 0.9 | 3.6 | 1.4 ± 3.8 | 15.4 | 1.6 ± 2.2 | 5.0 | 5.3 ± 7.0 | 20.6 | 4.24 |

[a] $p < 0.05$
[b] $p < 0.01$
[c] $p < 0.001$

acetates) than the other substrates. Saguaro and senita are distinguishable because the former has higher concentrations of acetoin while the latter is higher in n-butyric acid and 1-propanol. Organ pipe is different from agria in that the average concentration of acetic acid is significantly less. The conclusion based on these data is that volatile patterns present in the different substrates are demonstrably different.

## Volatile Production

Differences in plant chemistry provide a reasonable explanation for differences in certain volatiles. For example, agria and organ pipe rots have much higher concentrations of ethanol than the other substrates and are the only cacti that contain triterpene glycosides. The sugars, glucose and rhamnose (but not the aglycones), of these compounds are selectively consumed during the rotting process (Kircher 1982a), and these sugars are then fermented to produce the alcohol. This fact has been recently substantiated by a study of the volatiles produced by bacteria and yeasts when grown in media containing fractions of organ pipe cactus as the sole carbon source (Williams 1985). Approximately 70% of the volatiles detected in natural organ pipe rots are produced when cactus microorganisms are grown in triterpene glycoside medium. The same microorganisms produce few, if any, volatiles in media containing either the lipid or insoluble residue fractions even though the microbes were able to use these fractions as a carbon source. It appears, therefore, that the volatile patterns are determined primarily by plant chemistry.

## Attractiveness of Volatiles

Do the cactophilic *Drosophila* respond to volatile patterns in a manner which would explain their high substrate specificity? This question has been investigated using *D. mojavensis,* and the answer is affirmative. Field observations indicate that *D. mojavensis* has a strong preference for agria rots even when suitable organ pipe rots are available (Fellows and Heed 1972). In a series of substrate choice experiments, Robert Downing (1985) confirmed the preference of *D. mojavensis* for agria over organ pipe and for either of these cacti over other substrates. Necrotic cactus tissue was produced in the laboratory using cactus microorganisms and subsequently placed in traps inside a large Plexiglas box ($910 \times 380 \times 260$ cm). Approximately 400 flies per replication were introduced into the box, and the number of *D. mojavensis* caught in each trap after 24 hours was recorded. Results of this experiment using agria and organ pipe are shown in Table 1.7. The average preference for agria was 271 (78%) to 79 (22%). These numbers

Table 1.7. Substrate selection by *D. mojavensis* (data taken from Downing 1985)

| Replicate | N | Number Trapped by Necrotic Tissue | | N | Number Trapped by Volatile Solution | |
|---|---|---|---|---|---|---|
| | | Agria No. (%) | Organ Pipe No. (%) | | Agria No. (%) | Organ Pipe No. (%) |
| 1 | 420 | 291 (79) | 79 (21) | 403 | 290 (90) | 34 (10) |
| 2 | 402 | 275 (76) | 87 (24) | 419 | 229 (94) | 15 (6) |
| 3 | 370 | 227 (81) | 55 (19) | 416 | 295 (78) | 85 (22) |
| 4 | 406 | 292 (76) | 94 (24) | 417 | 340 (88) | 46 (12) |
| Average | | 271 (78) | 79 (22) | | 289 (87) | 45 (13) |

are significantly different from expected numbers based on a null hypothesis of no preference ($X^2 = 425.6$, df = 3, P $<<$ .001). Results of control experiments indicate that *D. mojavensis* exhibit no preference between fresh (unrotted) tissue of the two cacti (average percentage trapped = 52% and 48% for fresh agria and organ pipe respectively, $X^2 = 1.06$, df = 3, P $>$ .05). The concentration of volatiles in the necrotic tissues was subsequently determined by gas chromatography, and two solutions of volatiles were synthesized based on the GC analysis. These solutions were checked for accuracy by gas chromatography and used in another series of choice experiments. As can be seen in Table 1.7, *D. mojavensis* exhibit the same behavioral preference when given a choice between two solutions, one having a volatile pattern which mimics necrotic agria and the other which mimics necrotic organ pipe, as when given a choice between agria and organ pipe rots. The average preference was 289 (87%) for agria solution and 45 (13%) for organ pipe solution ($X^2 = 333.4$, df = 3, P $<<$ .001). These data provide strong support for the contention that volatiles are the chemical basis of host plant selection for *D. mojavensis*.

## CONCLUSIONS

This chapter reviews the chemical interactions between cacti and cactophilic *Drosophila* that play a role in host plant specificity. Two major conclusions emerge: (1) cactus stem chemistry is a primary determinant of host plant utilization by the four endemic *Drosophila* species and (2) stem chemistry probably also determines the volatile patterns produced in rots characteristic to each species of cactus. Differences in these patterns have been implicated, at least in one species, as the chemical basis of host plant selection by desert *Drosophila*.

## ACKNOWLEDGMENTS

The authors would like to thank John C. Williams and Robert J. Downing for the use of their unpublished data. This work was supported by a NSF grant (BSR 8207056) to W. B. Heed and J. C. Fogleman and by a NIH grant (GM34820) to Fogleman.

The chapter is dedicated in memory of Professor Henry Kircher who contributed the basic knowledge of the chemistry of the cacti of the Sonoran Desert. His wide range of interest in biological systems in general stimulated both colleagues and students.

## REFERENCES

Alcorn, S. M., May, C. 1962. Attrition of a saguaro forest. *Plant Dis. Rep.* 46:156–58.

Bagley, S. T., Seidler, R. J., Talbor, H. W., Morrow, J. E. 1978. Isolation of Klebsielleae from within living wood. *Appl. Environ. Microbiol.* 36:178–85.

Barker, J. S. F., Starmer, W. T., eds., 1982. *Ecological Genetics and Evolution: The Cactus-Yeast-Drosophila Model System.* Australia: Academic Press. 362 pp.

Barrows, W. M. 1907. The reaction of the pomace fly, *Drosophila ampelophila* Loew, to odorous substances. *J. Exp. Zool.* 4:515–37.

Begg, M., Hogben, F. R. S. 1946. Chemoreceptivity of *Drosophila melanogaster. Proc. Roy. Soc.* 133(ser. B): 1–19.

Begon, M. 1982. Yeasts and *Drosophila.* In *The Genetics and Biology of* Drosophila. Vol. 3b, eds. M. Ashburner, H. L. Carson, J. N. Thompson, Jr., 345–84. London: Academic Press.

Boyle, A. M. 1949. Further studies of the bacterial necrosis of the giant cactus. *Phytopathol.* 39:1029–52.

Brazner, J., Aberdeen, V., Starmer, W. T. 1984. Host-plant shifts and adult survival in the cactus breeding *Drosophila mojavensis. Ecol. Entomol.* 9:375–81.

Brown, S. D., Hodgkins, J. E., Massingill, J. L., Jr., Reinecke, M. G. 1972. The isolation, structure, synthesis and absolute configuration of the cactus alkaloid gigantine. *J. Org. Chem.* 37:1825–28.

Campbell, C. E., Kircher, H. W. 1980. Senita cactus: a plant with interrupted sterol biosynthetic pathways. *Phytochem.* 19:2777–79.

Djerassi, C., Brewer, H. W., Clark, C., Durham, L. J. 1962. Alkaloid studies—XXXVIII. Pilocereine—a trimeric cactus alkaloid. *J. Am. Chem. Soc.* 79:2203–10.

Downing, R. J. 1985. *The chemical basis for host plant selection in* Drosophila mojavensis. M. S. thesis. Univ. of Denver, Denver, CO.

Fellows, D. P., Heed, W. B. 1972. Factors affecting host plant selection in desert-adapted *Drosophila. Ecology* 53:850–58.

Fogleman, J. C. 1982. The role of volatiles in the ecology of cactophilic *Drosophila. See* Barker and Starmer (1982), 191–206.

———. 1984. The ability of cactophilic *Drosophila* to utilize soaked soil as larval substrates. *Droso. Inf. Ser.* 60:105–7.

Fogleman, J. C., Duperret, S. M., Kircher, H. W. 1986. The role of phytosterols in host plant utilization by cactophilic *Drosophila. Lipids* 21:92–96.

Fogleman, J. C., Hackbarth, K. R., Heed, W. B. 1981. Behavioral differentiation between two species of cactophilic *Drosophila*. III. Oviposition site preference. *Am. Nat.* 118:541–48.

Fogleman, J. C., Heed, W. B. 1981. A comparison of the yeast flora in the larval substrates of *D. nigrospiracula* and *D. mettleri*. *Droso. Inf. Ser.* 56:38–39.

Fogleman, J. C., Heed, W. B., Kircher, H. W. 1982. *Drosophila mettleri* and senita cactus alkaloids: fitness measurements and their ecological significance. *Comp. Biochem. Physiol.* 71(A): 413–17.

Fogleman, J. C., Kircher, H. W. 1986. Differential effects of fatty acid chain length on the viability of two species of cactophilic *Drosophila*. *Comp. Biochem. Physiol.* 83(A): 761–64.

Fogleman, J. C., Starmer, W. T. 1985. Analysis of the community structure of yeasts associated with the decaying stems of cactus. III. *Stenocereus thurberi*. *Microb. Ecol.* 11:165–73.

Fogleman, J. C., Starmer, W. T., Heed, W. B. 1981. Larval selectivity for yeast species by *Drosophila mojavensis* in natural substrates. *Proc. Natl. Acad. Sci.* 78:4435–39.

———. 1982. Comparisons of yeast florae from natural substrates and larval guts of southwestern *Drosophila*. *Oecologia* 52:187–91.

Gibson, A. C. 1982. Phylogenetic relationships of Pachycereeae. *See* Barker and Starmer (1982), 3–16.

Gibson, A. C., Horak, K. E. 1978. Systematic anatomy and phylogeny of Mexican columnar cacti. *Ann. Missouri Bot. Gard.* 65:999–1057.

Gilbert, D. G. 1980. Dispersal of yeasts and bacteria by *Drosophila* in a temperate forest. *Oecologia* 46:135–37.

Goodnight, K. C., Kircher, H. W. 1971. Metabolism of lathosterol by *Drosophila pachea*. *Lipids* 6:166–69.

Graf, P. A. 1965. *The relationship of* Drosophila nigrospiracula *and* Erwinia carnegieana *to the bacterial necrosis of* Carnegiea gigantea. M.S. thesis. Univ. of Arizona, Tucson.

Graham, D. C. 1964. Taxonomy of the soft rot coliform bacteria. In *Annual Review of Phytopathology*. Vol. 2, eds. J. G. Horsfall, K. F. Baker, 13–42. California: Annual Reviews.

Heed, W. B. 1977. A new cactus-feeding but soil-breeding species of *Drosophila* (Diptera: Drosophilidae). *Proc. Ent. Soc. Wash.* 79:649–54.

———. 1978. Ecology and genetics of Sonoran Desert *Drosophila*. In *Ecological Genetics: The Interface*. Ed. P. F. Brussard, 109–26. New York: Springer-Verlag. 247 pp.

———. 1982. The origin of *Drosophila* in the Sonoran Desert. *See* Barker and Starmer (1982), 65–80.

Heed, W. B., Kircher, H. W. 1965. Unique sterol in the ecology and nutrition of *Drosophila pachea*. *Science* 149:758–61.

Heed, W. B., Mangan, R. L. 1986. Community ecology of the Sonoran Desert *Drosophila*. In *The Genetics and Biology of Drosophila*. Vol. 3E, eds. M. Ashburner, H. L. Carson, J. N. Thompson, Jr., 311–45. London: Academic Press.

Heed, W. B., Starmer, W. T., Miranda, M., Miller, M. W., Phaff, H. J. 1976. An analysis of the yeast flora associated with cactophilic *Drosophila* and their host plants in the Sonoran Desert and its relation to temperate and tropical associations. *Ecology* 57:151–60.

Holzschu, D. L., Phaff, H. J. 1982. Taxonomy and evolution of some ascomycetous cactophilic yeasts. *See* Barker and Starmer (1982), 127–41.

Howard, D. J., Bush, G. L., Breznak, J. A. 1985. The evolutionary significance of bacteria associated with *Ragoletis*. *Evolution* 39:405–17.

Hutner, S. H., Kaplan, H. M., Enzmann, E. V. 1937. Chemicals attracting *Drosophila*. *Am. Nat.* 71:575–81.

Kalunta, C. I. 1982. *The bacterial ecology of* Drosophila pachea *and its host plant,* Lophocereus schottii. M.S. thesis. California State Univ., Los Angeles.

Kircher, H. W. 1977. Triterpene glycosides and queretaroic acid in organ pipe cactus. *Phytochem.* 16:1078–80.

———. 1980. Triterpenes in organ pipe cactus. *Phytochem.* 19:2707–12.

———. 1982a. Chemical composition of cacti and its relationship to Sonoran Desert *Drosophila. See* Barker and Starmer (1982), 143–58.

———. 1982b. Sterols and insects. In *Cholesterol Systems in Insects and Animals.* Ed. J. Dupont. Boca Raton, FL: CRC Press. 160 pp.

Kircher, H. W., Bird, H. L. 1982. Five 3β, 6α-dihydroxysterols in organ pipe cactus. *Phytochem.* 21:1705–10.

Kircher, H. W., Heed, W. B., Russell, J. S., Grove, J. 1967. Senita cactus alkaloids: their significance to Sonoran Desert ecology. *J. Insect Physiol.* 13:1869–74.

Lightle, P. C., Standring, E. T., Brown, J. G. 1942. A bacterial necrosis of the giant cactus. *Phytopathol.* 32:303–13.

Mangan, R. L. 1982. Adaptations to competition in cactus breeding *Drosophila. See* Barker and Starmer (1982), 257–72.

Meneley, J. C., Stanghellini, M. E. 1975. Establishment of an inactive population of *Erwinia carotovora* in healthy cucumber fruit. *Phytopathol.* 65:670–73.

Meyer, J. M., Fogleman, J. C. 1987. Significance of saguaro cactus alkaloids in the ecology of *Drosophila mettleri*, a soil-breeding, cactophilic drosophilid. *J. Chem. Ecol.* 13:2069–81.

Patterson, J. T., Crow, J. F. 1940. Hybridization in the mulleri group of *Drosophila. Univ. Tex. Publ.* 4032:251–56.

Patterson, J. T., Wheeler, M. R. 1942. Description of new species of the subgenera *Hirtodrosophila* and *Drosophila. Univ. Tex. Publ.* 4213:62–109.

Perombelon, M. C. M., Kelman, A. 1980. Ecology of the soft rot erwinias. In *Annual Review of Phytopathology.* Vol. 18, eds. R. G. Grogan, G. A. Zentmyer, E. B. Cowling, 361–87. California: Annual Reviews.

Phaff, H. J., Starmer, W. T. 1980. Specificity of natural habitats for yeasts and yeast-like organisms. In *Biology and Activities of Yeasts.* Eds. F. A. Skinner, S. M. Passmore, R. R. Davenport, 79–102. New York: Academic Press. 310 pp.

Purcell, A. H. 1982. Insect vector relationships with procaryotic plant pathogens. In *Annual Review of Phytopathology.* Vol. 20, eds. R. G. Grogan, G. A. Zentmyer, E. B. Cowling, 397–417. California: Annual Reviews.

Reed, M. R. 1938. The olfactory reactions of *Drosophila melanogaster* Meigen to the products of fermenting bananas. *Physiol. Zool.* 11:317–25.

Rosenzweig, M. L. 1979. Optimal habitat selection in two-species competitive systems. *Fortschr. Zool.* 25:283–93.

Starmer, W. T. 1981a. An analysis of the fundamental and realized niche of cactophilic yeasts. In *The Fungal Community: Its Organization and Role in the Ecosystem.* Eds. D. T. Wicklow, G. Carroll, 129–156. New York: Dekker. 864 pp.

———. 1981b. The evolutionary ecology of yeasts found in the decaying stems of cacti. In *Proceedings of the Fifth International Symposium on Yeasts.* Eds. G. G. Stewart, I. Russell, 493–98. Toronto: Pergamon of Canada Ltd.

———. 1981c. A comparison of *Drosophila* habitats according to the physiological attributes of the associated yeast communities. *Evolution* 35:38–52.

———. 1982a. Analysis of the community structure of yeasts associated with the decaying stems of cactus. I. *Stenocereus gummosus. Microb. Ecol.* 8:71–81.

———. 1982b. Associations and interactions among yeasts, *Drosophila* and their habitats. *See* Barker and Starmer (1982), 159–74.

Starmer, W. T., Barker, J. S. F., Phaff, H. J., Fogleman, J. C. 1986. Adaptations of *Drosophila* and yeasts: their interactions with the volatile 2-propanol in the cactus-microorganism-*Drosophila* model system. *Aust. J. Biol. Sci.* 39:69–77.

Starmer, W. T., Fogleman, J. C. 1986. Coadaptation of *Drosophila* and yeasts in their natural habitat. *J. Chem. Ecol.* 12:1037–55.

Starmer, W. T., Kircher, H. W., Phaff, H. J. 1980. Evolution and speciation of host plant specific yeasts. *Evolution* 34:137–46.

Starmer, W. T., Phaff, H. J. 1983. Analysis of the community structure of yeasts associated with the decaying stems of cactus. II. *Opuntia* species. *Microb. Ecol.* 9:247–59.

Starmer, W. T., Phaff, H. J., Miranda, M., Miller, M. W., Heed, W. B. 1982. The yeast flora associated with the decaying stems of columnar cacti and *Drosophila* in North America. *Evol. Biol.* 14:269–95.

Steenbergh, W. F. 1970. Rejection of bacterial rot by adult saguaro cacti (*Cereus giganteus*). *J. Ariz. Acad. Sci.* 6:78–81.

Turner, R. M., Brown, D. E. 1982. Sonoran desertscrub. *Desert Plants* 4:181–221.

Vacek, D. C. 1979. *The microbial ecology of the host plants of* Drosophila mojavensis. Ph.D. dissertation. Univ. of Arizona, Tucson.

———. 1982. Interactions between microorganisms and cactophilic *Drosophila* in Australia. *See* Barker and Starmer (1982), 175–90.

West, A. S. 1961. Chemical attractants for adult *Drosophila* species. *J. Econ. Entomol.* 54:677–81.

Williams, J. C. 1985. *The role of triterpene glycosides in the production of volatiles in the necrotic tissue of organpipe cactus.* M.S. thesis. Univ. of Denver, Denver, CO.

Young, D. J., Vacek, D.C., Heed, W. B. 1981. The facultatively anaerobic bacteria as a source of alcohols in three breeding substrates of cactophilic *Drosophila*. *Dros. Inf. Ser.* 56:165–66.

# 2

# HARVESTER ANTS AND HORNED LIZARDS PREDATOR-PREY INTERACTIONS

Patricia J. Schmidt

University of Arizona
Tucson, Arizona

and

Justin O. Schmidt

Southwestern Biological Institute
Tucson, Arizona

Of any known arthropod, harvester ants (Fig. 2.1) in the genus *Pogonomyrmex* have the most lethally toxic venom to mammals (Schmidt and Blum 1978; Schmidt and Schmidt, unpublished). This highly successful new world genus contains large ants that conspicuously dominate many of the arid regions of North America. Partly as a result of their visibility and abundance, harvester ants have been the subjects of numerous ecological (Kirkham and Fisser 1972; Rogers and Lavigne 1974; Whitford and Ettershank 1975; Davidson 1977; Harrison and Gentry 1981; Mandel and Sorenson 1982), population (Lavigne 1969; Rogers, Lavigne, and Miller 1972; MacKay 1981), natural history (Cole 1932; Wray 1938; Michener 1942; Willard and Crowell 1965; Whitford 1978), behavioral (Hölldobler 1971, 1976; Rogers 1974; Whitford, Johnson, and Ramirez 1976; Davidson 1978; Porter and Jorgensen 1981; Jorgensen and Porter 1982; Mintzer 1982; Gordon 1983a, 1983b, 1986), resource competition (Bernstein 1974, 1979; Hansen 1978; De Vita 1979; Mehlhop and Scott 1983), genetic (Johnson et al. 1969; Tomaszewski, Schaffer, and Johnson 1973), and even control (Killough and Le Sueur 1953; Crowell 1963; Borth 1986) studies. Several books (McCook

Figure 2.1.    Worker *Pogonomyrmex occidentalis* harvester
ant. Photograph by Hayward Spangler.

1879, 1882; Cole 1968) and an annotated bibliography (Lavigne and Rogers 1974) have been written about *Pogonomyrmex*.

Compared to harvester ants, horned lizards (*Phrynosoma*, [Iguanidae])
are rarely seen, being inconspicuous, secretive animals occurring in low
densities relative to their dominant saurid relatives. These unusually broad
and flattened lizards (Fig. 2.2) represent a striking morphological depar-
ture from the usual lizard template. They too have been subject to much
human interest, ranging from their unfortunate capture as pets to natural
history (Milne and Milne 1950), ecological (Tanner and Krogh 1973; Pianka
and Parker 1975; Montanucci 1981) behavioral (Lynn 1965; Tollestrup 1981;
Munger 1984b, 1984c; Powell and Russell 1985a), and nutritional (Powell
and Russell 1985b; Munger 1984a) studies. Their biology is summarized
in a recent book by Sherbrooke (1981).

Both harvester ants and horned lizards are dietary specialists. Harvester ants eat predominantly seeds from a variety of annual and perennial
plants; horned lizards, with a few exceptions, eat predominantly ants.
This ant eating by horned lizards set the biological stage for this study.
In this chapter, we analyze some of the adaptations that led to the ecological success of harvester ants, some biological and physiological properites
of horned lizards that have allowed this group to become ant specialists,
and how these two groups appear to be in a predator-prey evolutionary
interaction.

Figure 2.2.   Horned lizard *Phrynosoma cornutum*. Photograph by Wade Sherbrooke.

## HARVESTER ANTS

Three ant genera, all within the subfamily Myrmicinae (Formicidae),
are known to contain species that specialize in harvesting seeds as a major
food resource. A fourth genus, *Novomessor*, contains ants that sometimes
collect seeds. Three of these seed-collecting genera, *Pheidole*, *Veromessor*,
and *Novomessor*, possess blunt, nonpiercing sting apparatuses. The fourth
genus of seed-harvesting ants, the *Pogonomyrmex*, possess a strong piercing sting apparatus and an associated highly toxic venom (Fig. 2.3). In most
of the dry western and warm areas of North America, *Pogonomyrmex* is
the conspicuous and dominant group of seed-harvesting ants. In fact, in
many western areas they constitute the dominant ant species in the environment. For the remainder of this chapter, the term *harvester ant* will
refer only to the genus *Pogonomyrmex*.

*Pogonomyrmex* (excluding the subgenus *Ephebomyrmex*) are readily
recognized on the basis of their large size (6–9 mm), the presence of a
psammophore or "beard" of long stiff setae on the ventral portion of the
head and on the mandibles that aids in transporting small seeds and soil
particles (Spangler and Rettenmeyer 1966), and their generally reddish
color (in some areas, species such as *P. rugosus* appear black and other
species sometimes have dark heads or abdomens). They often construct

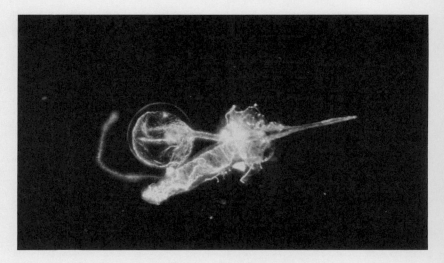

Figure 2.3.    Dissected view of a *Pogonomyrmex badius* sting apparatus. The sting shaft is used to penetrate the integument of the target organism and the venom from the spherical reservoir is injected through the sting shaft. The cylindrical gland below the venom reservoir is the Dufour's gland and is not used for defense.

conspicuous mounds that may be either cone shaped, dome shaped, or flat and are frequently surrounded by an area cleared of vegetation by the ants (Fig. 2.4). These characteristics of *Pogonomyrmex* are not universal and are only a generalization for the eight dominant species observed in various major habitats. Some species are small (3–5 mm) and secretive, have small colony populations, and lack noticeable mounds. For detailed taxonomic treatment of ants in general the reader is referred to Creighton (1950), for the ants of specific geographical areas to Wheeler and Wheeler (1963, 1973), and for *Pogonomyrmex* to Cole (1968). One definitive means of identifying a member of the genus *Pogonomyrmex* is by one's reaction to its sting. No other North American stinging ant (or bee or wasp) species is capable of inflicting lingering, excruciating pain that usually lasts 1–12 hours. Other diagnostic properties of harvester ant stings include localized sweating at the sting site, erection of the hairs around the sting site, often a dull, unpleasant pain in axial lymph nodes, and sometimes the presence of the sting apparatus in the wound (Schmidt 1983; Wheeler and Wheeler 1973).

The taxonomy of harvester ants has undergone periodic revision, and new

Figure 2.4. Colony nest mounds of harvester ants: *a, P. badius; b, P. occidentalis; c, P. owyheei (P. salinus* looks similar); *d, P. barbatus; e, P. rugosus; f, P. maricopa* from Willcox; *g, P. californicus;* and *h, P. desertorum.*

species have been described recently. At present in the United States there are 24 species organized in four species groups. Two of these species *P. angergismus* and *P. coli*, are workerless parasites of *P. rugosus*. In addition to the 24 U.S. species, *P. wheeleri*, the largest of all harvester ant species, lives in the Mexican states of Sinaloa, Nayarit, and Oaxaca. The most conspicuous mound-building species of harvester ants are *P. badius* occurring in the coastal plains of the southeastern United States; *P. barbatus and P. rugosus* mainly occurring in the stony-hard soil areas of Texas to Kansas and the hot areas of western United States and adjoining Mexico; *P. occidentalis, P, owyheei,* and *P. salinus* mainly occurring in the short and tall grass prairies and the sagebrush Great Basin areas of the United States; and *P. maricopa* and *P. californicus* often located in sandy or soft soil areas of the hot southwestern deserts of California, Arizona, New Mexico, Texas, and adjoining areas in Mexico (Fig. 2.4). The remaining 16 U.S. species are generally less abundant or are inconspicuous in their habitat, or they have small geographic ranges. Most of the research on harvester ants has been conducted on members of the eight dominant species listed above, plus *P. desertorum,* a small, abundant species that has unaggressive (to humans) habits, small colonies, and inconspicuous nest entrances (Fig. 2.4).

As the common name suggests, most species of harvester ants and all of the eight dominant species forage mainly for seeds of annual and perennial plants. They also collect pieces of dead arthropods, bird feces, and inedible plant materials and pebbles; the latter are often placed on the surface of the nest mound (Jorgensen and Porter 1982). Harvester ants can also be opportunistic predators, though this behavior is not strongly developed, and they are not attracted to nectar, other sweets or honeydew-secreting Homoptera. For more detailed information on the biology of harvester ants the reader is referred to McCook (1879, 1882), Wheeler (1910), Cole (1932, 1968), and Michener (1942).

Harvester ants possess a number of characteristics which make them susceptible to predation. Their colonies often contain large populations, for example, 10,000–20,000 individuals per colony in *P. rugosus* (MacKay 1981), making their activities conspicuous. Harvester ant colonies are long-lived, with reports of the same colonies surviving for 10–20 or more years (Michener 1942; Sharp and Barr 1960; Keeler 1982; Porter and Jorgensen 1988) as are adult individuals within the colonies. As an example of adult longevity, queenless colonies of *P. badius* have survived 18 months in the laboratory (J. O. Schmidt, unpublished) and underground brood-rearing and housekeeping activities (as well as inactivity) typically last about a year from adult eclosion before foraging commences (Porter and Jorgensen

1981). Overall, colonies of harvester ants form a stationary, concentrated source of edible individuals, a potential bonanza for predators.

## Harvester Ant Defenses

Harvester ants are well defended against most predators. Primary defenses include their strong mandibles, potent sting, hard exoskeleton, and their mandibular gland allomones/pheromones. The mandibles are effective weapons used against many potential arthropod predators, especially other ant species. Appendages and even major body parts of ants and other small assailants can be severed with the mandibles. The mandibles can also be "locked" onto powerful or large predators (Fig. 2.5). Sometimes a surviving assailant has attached to it a dried head from a harvester ant that had bitten it (Fig. 2.6). When an assailant is attacked, the mandibles also serve to anchor the ant and allow it to obtain the leverage necessary to drive the sting into the flesh. The sting is primarily effective as a defense against vertebrate predators. For further discussion of the use of harvester ant venoms in general as defenses against vertebrate predators, see Schmidt and Blum (1978) and Schmidt (1986, in press).

The hard integument of harvester ants stops penetration to vital areas by many of the assailants' weapons. This protection often affords the time necessary to employ or initiate defenses against the assailant. In the case of the harvester ants, active or physical defenses are the mandibles, sting, and chemical defenses. This last defense is the ketonic secretion (McGurk et al. 1966) produced by the mandibular glands of all castes of all species of harvester ants (J. O. Schmidt, unpublished). This ketonic secretion (mainly 4-methyl-3-heptanone) when placed in contact with living tissues causes pain (personal experience), and when the ant is taken into the assailant's mouth and crushed, this secretion may produce a noxious taste. The mandibles act in concert with the mandibular gland allomones by creating the wound into which the toxic secretion flows.

Other harvester ant defenses against predators are primarily physiological and behavioral. When one or a few individuals of a harvester ant colony are threatened near the colony, alarm pheromones are released. These pheromones consist of the same mandibular gland components (McGurk et al. 1966; Benthuysen and Blum 1974) that act as allomones, plus some compounds produced in the venom reservoirs (J. O. Schmidt et al., unpublished). When released these pheromones alert other colony members that a threat exists and help recruit defenders to mount a mass attack. If the stinging and mobbing behavior do not prevent severe forager depredation, then the colony defends itself another way—its workers stop foraging and close the entrance to the nest. This cessation of foraging can last

Figure 2.5. *P. rugosus* worker biting a *Ph. solare*. Hayward Spangler photograph.

Figure 2.6.    Head of *P. rugosus* still attached after two days
to the underside of *Ph. cornutum*.


several days or more and removes the reward for the predator which is no
longer stimulated to remain in the area (Gentry 1974; Whitford and Bryant
1979; MacKay 1982). Harvester ant colonies either clear vegetation from
the nest entrance, thereby increasing the risk of exposure of ant predators
to predation, or tend to have small, obscure nest entrances (Porter and
Jorgensen 1981). The deep (to 3 m or so, Lavigne 1969) subterranean nest
also helps protect the colony from predation (Porter and Jorgensen 1981).
One of the more novel defenses of harvester ants is to deprive the predator of the rich nutritional reward associated with successful prey inges-
tion. Harvester ants, like many other ant species, are in a unique position
to offer to predators those individuals with very little nutritious fat and
protein in comparison to bulk. Harvester ants accomplish this feat through
a strict behavioral progression of worker duties that vary with age. Young
protein-and-fat-rich workers inhabit the lower parts of the nest, often at
depths of 1–3 m below the surface (MacKay 1983, 1985; Porter and Jorgensen 1981) where they raise brood, tend to the queen, consume and
manipulate seeds, and act as a living reserve for the future. As the workers age, their body reserves shrink, and they move closer toward the surface of the nest (Porter and Jorgensen 1981; MacKay 1985). The final stage
of worker life, the time when they are old and their mandibles worn from

milling seeds is the time they emerge to the surface as part of the foraging force. This division of labor within a colony limits predation to exterior workers whose energy content is low, thus forming a "disposable caste" (Porter and Jorgensen 1981). These individuals are relatively "cheap," and the cost of their loss to predators is minimal for the colony. Because a predator must consume large numbers of these nutritionally deficient individuals to obtain meaningful nutrition, the capture of workers is not only less worthwhile but also is likely to be morphologically constraining on many predators: they simply do not have the stomach capacity to efficiently extract nutrients quickly enough from these bulky, chitinous prey.

## Predators of Harvester Ants

Reports of generalized predators of worker harvester ants are remarkably sparse. This alone attests to the general effectiveness of harvester ant defenses. Reported predators include mainly horned lizards among the vertebrates and to a lesser degree spiders (Table 2.1). *Sceloporus graciosus* might be a secondarily important vertebrate predator of harvester ants in the *P. occidentalis* complex, but the impact of their predation on harvester ants is unknown. Blind snakes (*Leptotyphlops dulcis*) eat both ant pupae (Stebbins 1985) and harvester ant workers (H. G. Spangler, personal communication). Other vertebrate predators of harvester ants are rare and of minor importance; most of these are isolated reports from stomach contents of birds or lizards. Many stomach analyses of a great diversity of species have been performed, and ants are frequently listed. Unfortunately, in these reports, taxonomic determinations as to genus were rarely made and, equally important, type of individuals is not listed (workers, reproductive alates, larvae). Not reporting caste can be especially misleading as, for example, in the data of McAtee (1932). In that study of 80,000 bird stomachs, 66 stomachs representing 25 avian species contained harvester ants, but the type of the consumed ants was not mentioned. Moreover the premier literature reference in that paper incorrectly described jackdaws (*Megaquiscalus*) as "cleaning up a colony in short time," when in actuality the original citation (Mitchell and Pierce 1912) stated "a colony of nesting jackdaws was observed to clean up an entire [mating] swarm in short time." The difference is crucial because alate ants are nutrient-rich, essentially defenseless individuals that are readily eaten by many predators. Unfortunately much of the literature data probably relates to consumption of alates, rather than workers.

A potential vertebrate predator that deserves more study is the flicker (*Colaptes*), a known predator of ants, especially formicine ants. In western Nebraska and Wyoming this bird is observed visiting mounds of *P.*

occidentalis during the morning hours when the sun has warmed the surface of the nest mounds, but the air is still cool. At this time the larvae are present just below the mound surface and flickers feed extensively on these larvae. Adult workers are not routinely observed in the crops of these foraging flickers (W. S. Moore, personal communication). The reason for the absence of adult workers in the flicker crop is unknown, but probably relates to both their nasty stings and their low nutrient density.

Spiders of the theridiid genera *Steatoda* (the cobweb spiders) and *Latrodectus* (the black widow spiders) can be important predators of harvester ants. These spiders often build webs over the entrances of harvester ant colonies and their depredations in severe situations cause the ants to shut down and stop foraging for several days (Hölldobler 1970; MacKay 1982). A variety of other spider species including the salticid ant specialist *Stoidis aurata* also take the occasional harvester ant. Sphecid wasps in the subgenus *Clypeadon* sting and paralyze worker harvester ants for the purpose of larval provisions in their nest. Although a dozen or so ants are captured for each larval cell, this harvester ant specialist is not common and probably has minimal impact on harvester ant populations (Evans 1962).

## HORNED LIZARDS

Horned lizards of the genus *Phrynosoma* are a group of highly derived lizards in the family Iguanidae. Because of their broad, squat shape, the horns at the back of their heads, their very short tails, and their relatively sluggish movement, these lizards are readily recognizable. They were originally considered to be members of the sceloporine lizard group, but they differ from the sceloporines in many characteristics. If, in fact, they are sceloporines, they are at best a very odd group (Etheridge 1964). Thus the *Phrynosoma* appear to be a unique genus without any close relatives.

Horned lizards live throughout most of western North America from the southern areas of the western three Canadian provinces, down the Pacific Coast, and southeast to Louisiana. In Mexico they extend to the Guatemalan border. Seven species, three of which have two or more subspecies, live in the United states and Canada. Six other species live in Mexico. Horned lizards are generally inhabitants of arid environments with sparse vegetation, and their habitat ranges in elevation from sea level to at least 3,410 m. The general biology, behavior and ecology of horned lizards is provided by Milne and Milne (1950), Pianka and Parker (1975), and Sherbrooke (1981).

Horned lizards have unusual food habits. Unlike most lizards that are general predators or herbivores, horned lizards specialize in ants as prey.

Table  2.1   Predators of *Pogonomyrmex* workers

| Predator Species | Prey Species | Nature of Predation | References |
|---|---|---|---|
| | Horned Lizards (*Phrynosoma*) | | |
| *Ph. douglassi* | *P. occidentalis* | 91 ants consumed in 1 hr | Knowlton 1938, 1946 |
| | *P. owyheei* | Many ants in 4 stomachs | Knowlton 1974a |
| *Ph. platyrhinos* | *P. occidentalis* | 89 ants consumed in 1 hr | Knowlton 1938, 1946 |
| | *P. occidentalis* | Many individuals in feces | Clarke and Comanor 1976 |
| | *P. owyheei* | Many ants in 4 stomachs | Knowlton 1974a |
| | *P. rugosus* | 5–10% of fecal pellets | Rissing 1981 |
| | *P. californicus* | 60–90% of fecal pellets | Rissing 1981 |
| *Ph. coronatum* | *P. californicus* | Fed almost entirely on one colony | Michener 1942 |
| | *P. barbatus* | 80% of 485 stomachs contained ants | Winton 1915 |
| *Ph. cornutum* | *P. rugosus, P. californicus, P. desertorum* | Main part of diet | Whitford and Bryant 1979 |
| | *P. desertorum* | Forages for short-term yield | Munger 1984a |
| *Ph. solare* | *P. rugosus* | Feeds almost exclusively on this sp. | Baharov 1975 |
| *Ph. mcalli* | *P. californicus* | 20–30% of diet | Turner and Medica 1982 |
| | *P. magnacanthus* | | Turner and Medica 1982 |
| | Other Lizards | | |
| *Sceloporus g. graciosus* | *P. occidentalis* | Many ants from 59 stomach samples | Knowlton 1942 |
| | | Many ants from 510 stomach samples | Knowlton 1947 |
| | | Ants from 10 stomach samples | Knowlton 1953 |
| | | 690 ants from 193 stomachs | Knowlton and Varcarce 1950 |
| | *P. owyheei* | 6.5 ants/lizard based on 114 lizards | Knowlton 1969 |
| *Uta stansburiana* | *P. occidentalis* | 17 ants in a stomach | Cole 1932 |
| | *P. owyheei* | Many ants from 125 stomachs | Knowlton 1974a |
| *Crotaphytus wislizenii* | *Pogonomyrmex* sp. | 2 ants in one stomach | Knowlton 1974a |
| *Leptotyphlops dulcis* | *P. rugosus* | Snake inserts head into nest and eats workers | H.G. Spangler, personal communication |
| | Birds | | |
| *Centrocercus urophasianus* | *P. occidentalis* | In stomachs | Knowlton and Thornley 1942 |
| *Colaptes cafer* | *P. occidentalis* | Large portion of stomach contents | Knowlton and Stains 1943 |
| *Oreoscoptes montanus* | *P. owyheei* | Ants in stomachs | Knowlton 1974b |
| *Sturnella neglecta* | *P. owyheei* | 2 ants in 11 stomachs | Knowlton 1974b |
| *Euphagus cyanocephalus* | *P. owyheei* | 7 ants in 2 stomachs | Knowlton 1974b |
| *Salpinctes o. obsoletus* | *P. occidentalis* | In stomachs | Knowlton and Harmston 1942 |
| *Spizella passerina arizonae* | *P. occidentalis* | Occasionally in stomachs | Knowlton and Harmston 1941 |
| *Amphispiza belli* | *P. owyheei* | Ants in stomachs | Knowlton 1974b |
| | Spiders | | |
| *Steatoda fulva* | *P. badius* | Captures ants in web over entrance | Holldobler 1970 |
| | *P. subnitidus* | Captures workers | MacKay 1982 |
| *S. pulcher* | *P. subnitidus* | Captures workers | MacKay 1982 |
| *Stoidis aurata* | *P. badius* | Ant specialist | Edwards, Carroll, and Whitcomb 1974 |
| *Latrodectus mactans* | *P. barbatus* | Captures workers | McCook 1879 |
| | *P. badius* | Occasional predator | Gentry 1974 |

Table 2.1 Predators of *Pogonomyrmex* workers (Continued)

| Predator Species | Prey Species | Nature of Predation | References |
|---|---|---|---|
| *Latrodectus hesperus* | *P. rugosus, P. subnitidus, P. montanus* | Captures workers | MacKay 1982 |
| *Euryopis coki* | *P. owyheei* | Attracts individuals near mound | Porter and Eastmond 1982 |
| *E. californicus* | *P. rugosus* | Captures workers | MacKay 1982 |
| *Xysticus* sp. | *P. rugosus* | Captures workers | MacKay 1982 |
| *Missonenops californicus* | *P. rugosus* | Captures ants in nearby plants | MacKay 1982 |
| *Argyrodes* sp. | *P. rugosus* | Captures workers | MacKay 1982 |

### Other Anthropods

| | | | |
|---|---|---|---|
| *Aphilanthops (Clypeadon) haigi* | *P. rugosus* | Paralyzes and provisions 14–16 workers per larval cell | Evans 1962 |
| *A. (C.)* sp. A | *P. rugosus* | 50 workers in nest; 11–12/cell | Evans 1962 |
| *A. (C.) dreisbachi + taurulus* | *P. rugosus* | Provisions with *Pogonomyrmex* | Evans 1962 |
| *A. (C.) sculleni* | *P. maricopa* | Provisions with *Pogonomyrmex* | Evans 1962 |
| *A. (C.) laticinctus* | *P. occidentalis* | 15–26 workers/cell provision | Evans 1962 |
| *A. (Listropygia) bechteli* | *P. californicus* | Provisions with *Pogonomyrmex* | Evans 1962 |
| *Apiomerus c. crassipes* | *P. badius* | Attacks lone foragers | Morrill 1975 |
| *Asilidae* sp. | *P.* sp. | Single observation | Whitford and Bryant 1979 |
| *Solpugidae* sp. | *P.* sp. | Single observation | Whitford and Bryant 1979 |

### Other

| | | | |
|---|---|---|---|
| *Dipodomys* sp. | *P. occidentalis* | Digs up and eats stored seeds | Clarke and Comanor 1973 |
| *Scaphiopus couchi* | *P. rugosus/ barbatus* | 74 workers in 15 stomachs | K. Tocque, personal communication |

They consume other small arthropods if available, but their main food is ants. The unusual broad, flat shape of horned lizards appears to be a consequence of their dietary specialization in ants. Their broad body form allows ample space for ingesting an enormous volume of chitinous and nutrient-poor ants. The stomach volume of *Ph. platyrhinos* is 13.4% of the body weight, a figure 65% greater than that of *Dipsosaurus dorsalis*, a vegetarian and the lizard with the largest stomach:body ratio of the other 14 North American lizards investigated (Pianka and Pianka 1970). Foraging for ants also requires of the lizard that it spend considerable time near ant colonies to obtain enough ants and that it must often adopt a "sit-and-wait" behavior in exposed situations. This kind of food specialization and the consequent body shape mean that the lizard can no longer make swift movements, especially for escape, and that the strategies of a cryptic pattern and behavior plus armored horns become the primary modes of defense. The Australian lizard, *Moloch horridus,* that feeds on ants, albeit not stinging ants, has a body shape as well as behaviors that are convergent to those of *Phrynosoma* (Pianka and Pianka 1970; Sherbrooke 1981).

## THE HORNED LIZARD AND HARVESTER ANT RELATIONSHIP

Harvester ants are frequently the dominant ants in their habitat. Certainly in many cases, they constitute the great bulk of diurnal biomass of arthropods on the soil surface and are readily available for foraging lizards. Despite their conspicuous presence, harvester ant workers, as mentioned earlier, have few predators. The notable exceptions are the horned lizards that not only specialize in preying on ants, but often specifically on harvester ants (Baharav 1975; Knowlton 1938; Rissing 1981; Turner and Medica 1982). Harvester ants may constitute up to 90% of the ants taken in fecal samples (Rissing 1981). How has this unusual situation arisen? We submit that it is not a coincidence, but rather the result of interactions between the ant prey and the lizard predators. During this process, most other meaningful predators of harvester ants have dropped out as the ants' defenses became too great to overcome. Only the most specialized predators like the horned lizards were able to keep up with the ants' ever-increasing defense capabilities. The consequence of this interaction was the evolution by the harvester ants of the world's most lethal arthropod venom and the evolution by horned lizards of a resistance to the effects of this venom.

## EVOLUTIONARY INTERACTION

### Harvester Ant Venom

Harvester ant venom contains a variety of vertebrate active compounds including the enzymes phospholipase A, hyaluronidase, lipase, esterase, acid phosphatase, and alkaline phosphatase, plus a potent hemolysin capable of directly destroying red blood cells (Schmidt and Blum 1978; Schmidt, Blum, and Overal 1986). In addition the venom induces extreme excruciating and long-lasting pain in humans that is more painfully debilitating than the venoms of the honeybee or all but one known ant venom (Schmidt 1983; J. O. Schmidt, unpublished). Interestingly the venom is not particularly lethal to other insects (Schmidt and Blum 1978). The venom of all 20 tested species of harvester ants is also extremely lethal to mice with intravenous $LD_{50}$ (median lethal dose) values ranging from 0.12 to 1.2 mg/kg (Schmidt and Blum 1978; Schmidt 1986; Schmidt and Schmidt, unpublished). Cowles and Bakker (1977) noted that horned lizards foraging for (honey) bees in the California desert seemed unaffected by the venom, though a line of stings was embedded inside their lips. Preliminary data indicated that horned lizards are much more resistant to harvester ant venom than are mice (Schmidt, Sherbrooke and Schmidt, 1989). In the following section we present the experimental details of our investigations into the nature of horned lizard resistance to harvester ant venom.

## Materials and Methods

*Pogonomyrmex rugosus* workers were collected from colonies near Willcox, Arizona, and Jim Hogg County, Texas; workers of *P. maricopa* were collected near Willcox, Arizona. Collected ants were stored at $-20°$ C until dissected. Pure venom was collected by dissecting venom reservoirs from surrounding tissues, rinsing them twice in distilled water to remove hemolymph, fat body, or other contaminants, and then rupturing the contents into a drop of distilled water (Schmidt 1986). Venoms were lyophilized and stored desiccated at $-20°$ C until used.

*Phrynosoma cornutum* and *Ph. modestum* were collected in the San Simon Valley, southern Arizona–New Mexico border; *Ph. douglassii* were collected near the top of the Santa Catalina Mountains, Arizona, a locality where *Pogonomyrmex* does not occur; *Sceloporus jarrovii* were from the Graham and Chiricahua mountains of Arizona; and the snakes *Lampropeltis getulus, Crotalus atrox*, and *Pituophis melanoleucus* were captured around Tucson, Arizona. Venoms of the honeybee (*Apis mellifera*), the eastern diamondback rattlesnake (*Crotalus adamanteus*), Russell's viper (*Vipera russelli*), and the Formosan cobra (*Naja naja atra*) were purchased from Sigma Chemical Company.

Lethality of *Pogonomyrmex* venom to mice and to *Phrynosoma* was determined by intravenous (iv) or intraperitoneal (ip) injection of sequentially doubled doses of venom in sale (0.85% NaCl) with the $LD_{50}$ calculated as in Schmidt, Blum, and Overal (1980). With the exception of the *P. rugosus* venom from Texas, which was used only for the ip lethality to mice, all venoms were from the Willcox, Arizona, ants.

Lizard blood samples were collected into Tris-buffered saline (TBS) (0.85% NaCl, 0.01 M Tris-HCl, pH 7.2, 0.01 M citrate) from decapitated adult lizards. Blood from *Lampropeltis getulus, Crotalus atrox, Pituophis melanoleucus*, and laboratory white mice was collected into heparinized or citrate-treated syringes by cardiac puncture. Blood from *Phrynosoma* and mice was stored at 4° C for less than seven days prior to erythrocyte removal and analysis. Plasma from the various blood samples was stored at $-20°$ C until used.

Hemolytic activity of *Pogonomyrmex maricopa* venom was determined using one ml samples of thrice-washed erythrocytes in TBS whose concentrations were adjusted to yield an absorbance of 0.8 at 545 nm when completely lysed. Graded doses of venom were added to the erythrocytic suspensions after which they were gently mixed and incubated for 30 minutes at 37° C. Hemolytic activity was quantified by centrifuging the suspension to sediment the cells, recording the absorbance of the supernatent at 545 nm and comparing this absorbance to that of a 100% hemolyzed sample. One hemolytic unit (HU) is the amount of test venom needed to release in 30 minutes the hemoglobin from 50% of the cells in a one ml suspension when incubated at 37° C (Schmidt, Blum, and Overal 1984).

The abilities of plasma from two species of lizards (*Ph. cornutum* and *S. jarrovii*) and three species of snakes (*L. getulus, C. atrox,* and *P. melanoleucus*) to neutralize *Pogonomyrmex maricopa* venom was detemined by intravenous injection into mice of graded amounts of plasma in saline mixed with the venom. To determine the ability of plasma of *Ph. cornutum* to neutralize the lethal effects of venoms in mice other than that of *Pogonomyrmex*, horned lizard plasma was mixed with the venoms and injected intravenously into mice. The venoms tested were from the rattlesnake *Crotalus adamanteus* (Crotalidae), the viper *Vipera russelli* Viperidae), the cobra *Naja naja atra* (Elapidae), and the honeybee *Apis mellifera* (Hymenoptera: Apidae). Mouse mortality within 24 hours was noted.

## Results

The lethalities of harvester ant venoms to laboratory mice and lizards are listed in Table 2.2. Both the venoms of *P. rugosus* and *P. maricopa* are extremely lethal by either iv or ip injection into mice. Of the two, *P. maricopa* venom appears to be almost four to six times more lethal to mice. On average, *P. maricopa* and *P. rugosus* from Willcox, Arizona, contain 25.0 µg venom/ant and 31.0 µg venom/ant respectively. Assuming most of an ant's venom is injected during a sting, one sting intravenously delivered could easily kill several 20.0 g mice.

Table 2.2 Lethalities of harvester ant venoms to mice and lizards (data mainly derived from Schmidt, Sherbrooke and Schmidt, 1989)

| Venom Source | Route Injected | Species Injected | Animals/ Dose | $LD_{50}$ (µg/g) | 95% CI (µg/g) |
|---|---|---|---|---|---|
| P. rugosus | iv | mice | 6 | 0.76 | 0.46–1.25 |
| | ip | mice | 6 | 0.47 | 0.20–1.11 |
| | ip | *Ph. douglassii* | 4 | >127 (24 hr) | — |
| | | | 6 | <64 (5 days) | — |
| P. maricopa | iv | mice | 6 | 0.19 | 0.072–0.197 |
| | ip | mice | 12 | 0.103 | 0.067–0.161 |
| | ip | *S. jarrovii* | 4 | 28 | 10–82 |
| | ip | *Ph. cornutum* | 4 | 162 | 61–432 |

In contrast to mice, all three species of lizards were much more resistant to harvester ant venom. The nine *Ph. douglassii*, all newly born, weighed from 1.1 to 2.2 g. When injected ip, none died in 24 hours or less in spite of receiving up to 127 μg venom/g lizard of *P. rugosus* venom, or approximately 270 times the dose mice could survive. The four lizards receiving 127 μg/g died between 2 and 4 days and those receiving 64 μg/g died between 3 and 5 days. The exact interpretation of this long-term data is unclear because the single saline control lizard died in 7 days. This preliminary evidence, showing that the lizards were clearly more resistant to the venom than mice, led us to further exploration of the horned lizard-harvester ant interaction.

*Sceloporus jarrovii*, though many times more resistant than mice to *P. maricopa* venom, was less resistant than horned lizards. In the case of *S. jarrovii*, seven of the lizards given 32–128 μg/g venom died within 24 hours, two more by the second day, and a final one on the fifth day. Even at the lowest dosage of 16 μg/g three of the four lizards became partially to severely paralyzed by 18 hours and remained that way for two days. After three days, two of the lizards were very dark colored and partially paralyzed. The last affected lizard did not totally regain its grayish color and normal behavior for over 10 days. Such long-term effects are not generally observed in mice: by the end of 24 hours, surviving mice are usually completely normal in appearance.

*Ph. cornutum* lives in the habitat of and is known to ingest *P. maricopa*. Four 27–35 g males received doses of 81 μg *P. maricopa* venom/g lizard. None exhibited any immediate sign of distress and only one lizard ever appeared at all affected. At 24 hours this lizard was somewhat reticent to run when prodded, but readily and vigorously righted itself and ran off when placed on its back. Two lizards weighing 31 (male) and 51 (female) g, respectively survived *P. maricopa* venom doses of 162 μg/g and two male lizards (31 and 43 g) died when challenged with that dose. The lizards that died exhibited no immediate profound symptoms of envenomation and appeared reasonably normal for a day or two, at which time their rear legs showed symptoms of paralysis. About a day before death, the lizards became almost totally paralyzed. Death occurred in 3 (43 g lizard) and 9 (31 g lizard) days. The two surviving lizards never exhibited severe symptoms of envenomation; their greatest symptoms were temporary loss of appetite and a partial paralysis of the rear legs from 2 to 3 days after injection, a symptom that gradually disappeared.

A single 29 g male lizard received an injection of 324 μg/g *P. maricopa* venom. Even at this dosage the lizard appeared reasonably normal for 4 days, but died the fifth day. The median lethal dose of venom (162 μg/g) to *Ph. cornutum* is nearly 1,600 times that which kills an average mouse (Table 2.2) and for a 31 g lizard represents the venom from 200 ants.

Because harvester ant venom is highly hemolytic to red blood cells of mammals (Bernheimer, Avigad, and Schmidt 1980), blood cell resistance in horned lizards is a conceivable means by which lizards are protected against lethal hemolysis. When washed erythrocytes (washing removes possible interfering plasma factors) of mice and Ph. cornutum and Ph. modestum were compared for resistance to hemolysis, very little difference was observed. The respective hemolytic units/mg P. maricopa venom were 167 for mice and 104 for each of the horned lizards (Schmidt, Sherbrooke, and Schmidt, in press). This indicates that the resistance of horned lizards is not erythrocyte based.

To determine if factors responsible for neutralizing Pogonomyrmex venom reside in the plasma of Phrynosoma blood, we took plasma from P. cornutum and compared it to the plasma of four other reptiles, the lizard S. jarrovii and the snakes L. getulus, C. atrox, and P. melanoleucus. In each species, plasma alone, and P. maricopa venom (approximately $2.5 \times LD_{50}$) mixed with plasma in graduated increasing doses was injected intravenously into mice (Table 2.3). All eight control mice that received venom but no plasma died. Groups of four and two mice that received only P. cornutum plasma (1.02 and 2.00 μl/g mouse) all survived with no signs of distress at any time. Mice receiving 0.39 or 0.41 μl plasma/g mouse died when also receiving 2.4 or 3.6 times an $LD_{50}$ dose respectively of P. maricopa venom. All mice receiving the same amount of venom plus double or quadruple the quantity of Ph. cornutum plasma survived without symptoms of envenomation.

Similar tests using plasma from the lizards and snakes were conducted to determine if adequate levels of their plasma, like Phrynosoma plasma, could protect mice from the lethal action of harvester ant venom. Both L. getulus and C. atrox plasma are known to have factors that resist the lethal effects of crotalid snake venoms (Rosenfeld and Glass 1940; Philpot and Smith 1950; Straight, Glenn, and Snyder 1976). Neither of these plasmas plus the other two test plasmas at levels double (for L. getulus and P. melanoleucus) or quadruple (for S. jarrovii and C. atrox) the level of Phrynosoma plasma that protects mice conferred any noticeable protection for mice envenomed by harvester ant venom. The times of death in mice with these added plasmas were virtually identical to those receiving venom only. Plasmas of L. getulus and C. atrox are known to be toxic in themselves to mice (Rosenfeld and Glass 1940; Philpot and Smith 1950; Straight, Glenn, and Snyder 1976). In our tests, the levels of these plasmas we used were below those known to be lethal. The top level of P. melanoleucus plasma in the controls was lethal to mice and no level below that appeared to confer any selective protection to mice.

Table 2.3 Comparative ability of reptile plasmas to neutralize the lethal effects of *Pogonomyrmex maricopa* venom intravenously injected into mice

| Treatment | Venom Values | | Plasma (µl/g Mouse) | Mortality (24 hr)/N |
|---|---|---|---|---|
| | $xLD_{50}$ | µg/g Mouse | | |
| Control | 2.3 | 0.28 | 0 | 8/8 |
| *Phrynosoma cornutum* | (Test 1)[1] | | | |
| Plasma only | 0 | 0 | 1.02 | 0/4 |
| Plasma + venom | 2.4 | 0.29 | 0.39 | 4/4 |
| Plasma + venom | 2.5 | 0.30 | 0.81 | 0/4 |
| Plasma + venom | 2.7 | 0.32 | 1.71 | 0/4 |
| | (Test 2) | | | |
| Plasma only | 0 | 0 | 2.00 | 0/2 |
| Plasma + venom | 3.6 | 0.43 | 0.41 | 4/4 |
| Plasma + venom | 3.6 | 0.43 | 0.83 | 0/4 |
| Plasma + venom | 3.6 | 0.43 | 1.67 | 0/4 |
| *Sceloporus jarrovii*[1] | | | | |
| Plasma only | 0 | 0 | 1.48 | 0/4 |
| Plasma + venom | 2.4 | 0.29 | 0.34 | 4/4 |
| Plasma + venom | 2.5 | 0.30 | 0.71 | 4/4 |
| Plasma + venom | 2.6 | 0.32 | 1.51 | 4/4 |
| Plasma + venom | 2.7 | 0.33 | 3.14 | 4/4 |
| *Lampropeltis getulus*[1] | | | | |
| Plasma only | 0 | 0 | 1.67 | 0/3 |
| Plasma + venom | 2.5 | 0.30 | 0.83 | 3/3 |
| Plasma + venom | 2.5 | 0.30 | 1.67 | 3/3 |
| *Crotalus atrox* | | | | |
| Plasma only | 0 | 0 | 3.6[1] | 50%[2] |
| Plasma + venom | 2.5 | 0.30 | 0.83 | 4/4 |
| Plasma + venom | 2.5 | 0.30 | 1.67 | 4/4 |
| Plasma + venom | 2.5 | 0.30 | 3.33 | 4/4 |
| *Pituophis melanoleucus* | | | | |
| Plasma only | 0 | 0 | 1.67 | 4/4 |
| Plasma + venom | 2.4 | 0.29 | 0.36 | 4/4 |
| Plasma + venom | 2.6 | 0.31 | 0.76 | 4/4 |
| Plasma + venom | 2.8 | 0.33 | 1.62 | 4/4 |

[1]Data from Schmidt, Sherbrooke, and Schmidt (1989).
[2]Data from Straight, Glenn, and Snyder (1976) and assuming plasma as 7% total dissolved solids by weight.

Plasma of *Phrynosoma* appeared unique among those tested in its ability to strongly neutralize the effects of harvester ant venom. To determine if this neutralizing ability extends to a variety of venoms or is limited to harvester ant venoms, the same and two times the amounts of *Ph. cornutum* plasma that confers protection in mice against *P. maricopa* venoms were admixed with the venoms of the honeybee and of snakes from three different families and injected into mice. The results are shown in Table 2.4. In no case did the *Ph. cornutum* plasma provide any protection against any of the other venoms. For each of the four non-ant venoms, doses twice the $LD_{50}$ were sought. In the case of *C. adamanteus* venom, the literature $LD_{50}$ value was 1.7 $\mu$g/g (Philpot and Smith 1950) but the rapid deaths of our animals caused us to reinvestigate this. The $LD_{50}$ in our tests was about half that; thus the actual doses of venom injected with plasma were higher than desired, a feature which complicates interpretation. The literature value of 0.29 $\mu$g/g (Minton and Minton 1980) for *Naja naja atra* was low for our venom. Based on our analysis, the lethality was approximately 0.55 $\mu$g/g.

## Discussion

Mice are clearly highly susceptible to the effects of harvester ant venom. Lizards are generally more resistant. The cause of this trend is unclear,

Table 2.4 Comparative ability of *Phrynosoma cornutum* plasmas to neutralize the lethal effects of various venoms intravenously injected into mice

| Venom Injected | Venom Values | | Plasma | Mortality |
| --- | --- | --- | --- | --- |
| | $xLD_{50}$ | $\mu$g/g Mouse | ($\mu$l/g Mouse) | (24 hr)/N |
| *Pogonomyrmex maricopa* | 2.3 | 0.28 | 0 | 8/8 |
| ($LD_{50}$ = 0.119 $\mu$g/g) | 2.4 | 0.29 | 0.39 | 4/4 |
| | 2.5 | 0.30 | 0.81 | 0/4 |
| | 2.7 | 0.32 | 1.71 | 0.4 |
| *Apis mellifera* | 2.8 | 8.0 | 0 | 4/4 |
| ($LD_{50}$ ≈ 2.84 $\mu$g/g)[1] | 2.8 | 8.0 | 0.83 | 4/4 |
| | 2.8 | 8.0 | 1.67 | 4/4 |
| *Crotalus adamanteus* | 4.8 | 3.9 | 0 | 4/4 |
| ($LD_{50}$ = 0.825 $\mu$g/g)[2] | 4.8 | 3.9 | 0.83 | 4/4 |
| | 4.8 | 3.9 | 1.67 | 4/4 |
| *Vipera russelli* | 2.0 | 0.50 | 0 | 4/4 |
| ($LD_{50}$ = 0.25 $\mu$g/g)[3] | 2.0 | 0.50 | 0.83 | 4/4 |
| | 2.0 | 0.50 | 1.67 | 4/4 |
| *Naja naja atra* | 2.1 | 1.16 | 0 | 4/4 |
| ($LD_{50}$ ≈ 0.55 $\mu$g/g)[3,4] | 2.1 | 1.16 | 0.83 | 4/4 |
| | 2.1 | 1.16 | 1.67 | 4/4 |

[1]Unpublished value for the venom used and our test animals (N = 8/dose; 95% CI = 1.97–4.10 $\mu$g/g).
[2]Unpublished value for the venom used and our test animals (N = 6/dose; 95% CI = 0.45–1.51 $\mu$g/g).
[3]Minton and Minton 1980.
[4]Unpublished value for the venom and our test animals (N = 6/dose; 95% CI = 0.346–0.864 $\mu$g/g).

but there are two major differences between mice and lizards. Mice are endothermic and, as such, must oxidatively generate much energy to maintain their body temperature. Anything which severely impairs the ability to breath, their heart's ability to circulate blood, or their ability to regulate body temperature leads to rapid death. In the case of mice envenomed with low doses of harvester ant venom, both respiratory movement and lung capacity are seriously impaired. Higher doses cause death within an hour or two. For reptiles, the amount of oxygen needed for the metabolism of these exothermic animals is minimal. Even a severely paralyzed animal stands a chance of surviving if slight respiration or passive diffusion of oxygen is possible and if the heart continues beating and all other factors are reasonably normal. How important this difference between mice and lizards is uncertain. The second difference between the two is taxonomic—they belong to rather different classes of vertebrates.

Even among the lizards, *Phrynosoma* appears to be uniquely resistant to the effect of harvester ant venom. The median lethal dose of *P. maricopa* venom in mature horned lizards is approximately six times that for *S. jarrovii* (Schmidt, Sherbrooke, and Schmidt, 1989). The dose of 81 $\mu$g/g delivered to *Ph. cornutum* produced no outwardly noticeable effects whereas doses five-fold lower severely impaired three of the four tested *S. jarrovii* (Schmidt, Sherbrooke and Schmidt, 1989). *Anoles* spp. of lizards were also paralyzed totally or partially for several days after receiving doses of *P. maricopa* venom of 13 $\mu$g/g; and a single *S. virgatus* died in 8–24 hours when given 62 $\mu$g/g of that venom (J. O. Schmidt unpublished data).

The ability of erythrocytes from two species of horned lizards to resist lysis by *P. maricopa* venom was similar to that of mouse erythrocytes (Schmidt, Sherbrooke, and Schmidt, 1989). Bernheimer, Avigad, and Schmidt (1980) studied the sensitivity of eleven mammals to *P. barbatus* venom and discovered a wide range of from 185 to 900 HU, an indication that the difference in our studies between mice and horned lizards is minor. We conclude that horned lizards receive little, if any, specific protection by *P. maricopa* venom attributable to erythrocytic resistance to lysis.

Of all the plasmas tested for ability to neutralize the lethal activity of *P. maricopa* venom, only that of *Phrynosoma* was effective. This is especially telling in light of the evidence that the plasma of both *Lampropeltis* and *Crotalus* have the ability to neutralize *Crotalus* venom (Rosenfeld and Glass 1940; Philpot and Smith 1950; Straight, Glenn, and Snyder 1976). *Sceloporus* plasma served mainly as a control "relative" of *Phrynosoma* to determine if lizards in general have neutralizing plasmas. The results indicate that the resistant factor(s) in snake blood are not broadly based enough in action to neutralize harvester ant venom and that only horned lizards possess a factor that can neutralize the activity of *Pogonomyrmex* venom.

The fact that *Phrynosoma* plasma could not neutralize the effects of representative venoms from the three major snake families or of the honeybee indicates that the neutralizing factor is apparently specific to harvester ant venom. Thus, this is the first known example of a vertebrate animal having a specific resistance to the venom of an arthropod.

## LIZARD-ANT EVOLUTION

Long-term evolutionary histories are impossible to reconstruct exactly. Based on evidence, we can, however, suggest reasonable scenarios. The geographic origin of harvester ants is unknown, but as either the climate changed and dried, or as they expanded their habitat tolerance, their ancestor adapted to arid environments. Meanwhile an ancestor of horned lizards either moved into or lived in this area. This lizard ancestor might already be feeding on nonvenomous formicine or dolichoderine ants, much as does *Moloch*, the Australian analogue of *Phrynosoma* (Pianka and Pianka 1970). At this point the lethal activity of the venom of the harvester ant ancestor and venom resistance of the horned lizard ancestor are unknown; presumably the lizard had no blood factor that resisted the ant's venom. The ant venom was likely much less lethal, probably around 2% the present activity of *P. maricopa* at Willcox and about the same as one of its nearest North American relatives, *Manica bradleyi* (Schmidt and Schmidt, unpublished data). Obvious responses of the ant ancestor to newly encountered lizard predation would be behavioral (mobbing and so on) and the evolution of a more lethal venom. Responses of the lizard ancestor would likely be behavioral (avoid high concentrations of ants and so forth) and the evolution of resistance to the ant's venom. Thus the defense-counterdefense interaction was underway.

An evolutionary predator-prey interaction between *Phrynosoma* and *Pogonomyrmex* appears to continue at present. *P. maricopa* at Willcox is the most lethal of all harvester ant venoms and is approximately four times as lethal as the average harvester ant venom (n = 20 tested species). *P. maricopa* at Willcox lives in a small geographic area inhabited by three desert horned lizard species (*Ph. cornutum*, *Ph. modestum*, and *Ph. solare*) and near the habitat of the mountain and high plains species *Ph. douglassi*. No place in the United States has more species of horned lizards. Among populations of *P. maricopa*, those at Willcox have especially lethal venoms: for example, populations living in Patagonia and in Tucson, Arizona, are only 25 and 16% as lethal respectively as the Willcox population (Schmidt and Schmidt unpublished data), and these populations face only at most one species of horned lizard.

## CONCLUSIONS

Harvester ants appear to have no meaningful predators other than horned lizards. Harvester ants also possess the most lethal known venom (to mice) of any animal in the New World. Horned lizards are slow, broad-bodied lizards that feed primarily on ants and especially on harvester ants. Horned lizards are essentially unique among lizards in that they have evolved the immense stomach and digestive tract that is necessary for feeding on bulky and mostly chitinous ant prey. Horned lizards are also exceedingly resistant to the venom of harvester ants. This resistance is at least in part the result of their possession of a blood factor(s) that specifically neutralizes the mouse-lethal activity of harvester ant venom, but fails to neutralize the lethal activities of snake or bee venoms. These discoveries indicate that harvester ants and horned lizards were and still are evolving as predator and prey.

## ACKNOWLEDGMENT

We thank Dr. James L. Jarchow whose talented ability and willingness to bleed snakes made much of this study possible, Stephen Buchmann, Hayward Spangler, and Wade Sherbrook for manuscript reviews and especially Wade Sherbrooke for collecting the lizard plasmas and providing invaluable assistance and suggestions throughout this research. Scientific collecting permits were provided by the Arizona Game and Fish Department.

## REFERENCES

Baharav, D. 1975. Movement of the horned lizard *Phrynosoma solare*. *Copeia* 1974:649–57.

Benthuysen, J. L., Blum, M. S. 1974. Quantitative sensitivity of the ant *Pogonomyrmex barbatus* to the enantiomers of its alarm pheromone. *J. Georgia Entomol. Soc.* 9:235–38.

Bernheimer, A. W., Avigad, L. S., Schmidt, J. O. 1980. A hemolytic polypeptide from the venom of the red harvester ant, *Pogonomyrmex barbatus*. *Toxicon* 18:271–78.

Bernstein, R. A. 1974. Seasonal food abundance and foraging activity in some desert ants. *Am. Nat.* 108:490–98.

———. 1979. Schedules of foraging activity in species of ants. *J. Anim. Ecol.* 48:921–30.

Borth, P. W. 1986. Field evaluation of several insecticides on maricopa harvester ant (Hymenoptera: Formicidae) colony activity in fallow southwestern Arizona cropland. *J. Econ. Entomol.* 79:1632–36.

Clarke, W. H., Comanor, P. L. 1973. The use of western harvester ant, *Pogonomyrmex occidentalis* (Cresson), seed stores by heteromyid rodents. *Biol. Soc. Nev. Occas. Papers* 34:1–6.

―――. 1976. The northern desert horned lizard, *Phrynosoma platyrhinos platyrinos*, as a predator of the western harvester ant, *Pogonomyrmex occidentalis*, and a dispersal agent for *Eriogonum baileyi. J. Idaho Acad. Sci.* 12:9–12.

Cole, A. C., Jr. 1932. The relation of the ant, *Pogonomyrmex occidentalis* Cr., to its habitat. *Ohio J. Sci.* 32:133–46.

―――. 1968. *Pogonomyrmex Harvester Ants.* Knoxville: University of Tennessee Press. 222 pp.

Cowles, R. B., Bakker, E. S. 1977. *Desert Journal Reflections of a Naturalist.* Berkeley: University of California Press. 263 pp.

Creighton, W. S. 1950. Ants of North America. *Bull. Mus. Comp. Zool. (Harvard)* 104:1–585.

Crowell, H. H. 1963. Control of the western harvester ant, *Pogonomyrmex occidentalis*, with poisoned baits. *J. Econ. Entomol.* 56:295–98.

Davidson, D. W. 1977. Species diversity and community organization in desert seed-eating ants. *Ecology* 58:711–24.

―――. 1978. Experimental tests of the optimal diet in two social insects. *Behav. Ecol. Sociobiol.* 4:35–41.

De Vita, J. 1979. Mechanisms of interference and foraging among colonies of the harvester ant *Pogonomyrmex californicus* in the Mojave Desert. *Ecology* 60:729–37.

Edwards, G. B., Carroll, J. F., Whitcomb, W. H. 1974. *Stoidis aurata* (Araneae: Salticidae), a spider predator of ants. *Florida Entomol.* 57:337–46.

Etheridge, R. 1964. The skeletal morphology and systematic relationships of sceloporine lizards. *Copeia* 1964:610–31.

Evans, H. E. 1962. A review of nesting behavior of digger wasps of the genus *Aphilanthops*, with special attention to the mechanics of prey carriage. *Behaviour* 29:239–60.

Gentry, J. B. 1974. Response to predation by colonies of the Florida harvester ant, *Pogonomyrmex badius. Ecology* 55:1328–38.

Gordon, D. M. 1983a. The relation of recruitment rate to activity rhythms in the harvester ant, *Pogonomyrmex barbatus* (F. Smith) (Hymenoptera: Formicidae). *J. Kansas Entomol. Soc.* 56:277–85.

―――. 1983b. Daily rhythms in social activities of the harvester ant, *Pogonomyrmex badius. Psyche* 90:413–23.

―――. 1986. The dynamics of the daily round of the harvester ant colony (*Pogonomyrmex barbatus*). *Anim. Behav.* 34:1402–19.

Hansen, S. R. 1978. Resource utilization and coexistence of three species of *Pogonomyrmex* ants in an Upper Sonoran grassland community. *Oecologia* 35:109–17.

Harrison, J. S., Gentry, J. B. 1981. Foraging pattern, colony distribution, and foraging range of the Florida harvester ant, *Pogonomyrmex badius. Ecology* 62:1467–73.

Hölldobler, B. 1970. *Steatoda fulva* (Theridiidae), a spider that feeds on harvester ants. *Psyche* 77:202–208.

―――. 1971. Homing in the harvester ant *Pogonomyrmex badius. Science* 171:1149–51.

―――. 1976. Recruitment behavior, home range orientation and territoriality in harvester ants, *Pogonomyrmex. Behav. Ecol. Sociobiol.* 1:3–44.

Johnson, F. M., Schaffer, H. E., Gillaspy, J. E., Rockwood, E. S. 1969. Isozyme genotype-environment relationships in natural populations of the harvester ant, *Pogonomyrmex barbatus*, from Texas. *Biochem. Genet.* 3:429–50.

Jorgensen, C. D., Porter, S. D. 1982. Foraging behavior of *Pogonomyrmex owyheei* in southeast Idaho. *Environ. Entomol.* 11:381–84.

Keeler, K. H. 1982. Preliminary report of colony survivorship in the western harvester ant (*Pogonomyrmex occidentalis*) in western Nebraska. *Southwest. Nat.* 27:245–46.

Killough, J. R., Le Sueur, H. 1953. The red harvester ant. *Our Public Lands (BLM)* 3(1): 4, 14.

Kirkham, D. R., Fisser, H. G. 1972. Rangeland relations and harvester ants in northcentral Wyoming. *J. Range Manag.* 25:55–60.

Knowlton, G. F. 1938. Horned toads in ant control. *J. Econ. Entomol.* 31:128.

———. 1942. Range lizards as insect predators. *J. Econ. Entomol.* 35:602.

———. 1946. Feeding habits of some reptiles. *Herpetologia* 3:77–80.

———. 1947. The sagebrush swift in pasture insect control. *Herpetologia* 4:25.

———. 1953. Some insect food en *Sceloporus g. graciosus* (B.-G.). *Herpetologia* 9:70.

———. 1969. Some insect food of Curlew Valley lizards. *Proc. Utah Acad. Sci.* 46:160–61.

———. 1974a. Arthropod food of Curlew Valley lizards. *Utah State Univ. Ecol. Center Terrestrial Arthropods Series,* no. 7, 1–7.

———. 1974b. Some terrestrial arthropod food of Curlew Valley birds. *Utah State Univ. Ecol. Center Terrestrial Arthropods Series*, no. 8, 1–15.

Knowlton, G. F., Harmston, F. C. 1941. Insect food of the chipping sparrow. *J. Econ. Entomol.* 34:123–24.

———. 1942. Insect food of the rock wren. *Great Basin Nat.* 3:22.

Knowlton, G. F., Stains, G. S. 1943. Flickers eat injurious insects. *Can. Entomol.* 75:118.

Knowlton, G. F., Thronley, H. F. 1942. Insect food of the sage grouse. *J. Econ. Entomol.* 35:107–8.

Knowlton, G. F., Valcarce, A. C. 1950. Insect food of the sagebrush swift in Box Elder County of Utah. *Herpetologia* 6:33–34.

Lavigne, R. J. 1969. Bionomics and nest structure of *Pogonomyrmex occidentalis* (Hymenoptera: Formicidae). *Ann. Entomol. Soc. Am.* 62:1166–75.

Lavigne, R. J., Rogers, L. E. 1974. An annotated bibliography of the harvester ants, *Pogonomyrmex occidentalis* (Cresson) and *Pogonomyrmex owyheei* Cole. *Univ. Wyoming Agr. Exp. Stn. Sci. Monog.* 26:1–18.

Lynn, R. T. 1965. A comparative study of display behavior in *Phrynosoma* (Iguanidae). *Southwest. Nat.* 10:25–30.

MacKay, W. P. 1981. A comparison of the nest phenologies of three species of *Pogonomyrmex* harvester ants (Hymenoptera: Formicidae). *Psyche* 88:25–74.

———. 1982. The effect of predation of western widow spiders (Araneae: Theridiidae) on harvester ants (Hymenoptera: Formicidae). *Oecologia* 53:406–11.

———. 1983. Stratification of workers in harvester ant nests (Hymenoptera: Formicidae). *J. Kansas Entomol. Soc.* 56:538–42.

———. 1985. A comparison of the energy budgets of three species of *Pogonomyrmex* harvester ants (Hymenoptera: Formicidae). *Oecologia* 66:484–94.

Mandel, R. D., Sorenson, C. J. 1982. The role of the western harvester ant (*Pogonomyrmex occidentalis*) in soil formation. *Soil Sci. Soc. Am. J.* 46:785–88.

McAtee, W. L. 1932. Effectiveness in nature of the so-called protective adaptations in the animal kingdom, chiefly as illustrated by the food habits of Nearctic birds. *Smithsonian Misc. Collect.* 85(7): 1–201.

McCook, H. C. 1879. *The Natural History of the Agricultural Ant of Texas*. Philadelphia: Acad. Nat. Sci. Phila. 311 pp.

———. 1882. *The Honey Ants of the Garden of the Gods, and the Occident Ants of the American Plains*. Philadelphia: J. B. Lippincott and Co. 188 pp.

McGurk, D. J., Frost, J., Eisenbraun, E. J., Vick, K., Drew, W. A., Young, J. 1966. Volatile compounds in ants: identification of 4-methyl-3-heptanone from *Pogonomyrmex* ants. *J. Insect Physiol.* 12:1435–41.

Mehlhop, P., Scott, N. J., Jr. 1983. Temporal patterns of seed use and availability in a guild of desert ants. *Ecol. Entomol.* 8:69–85.

Michener, C. D. 1942. The history and behavior of a colony of harvester ants. *Sci. Monthly.* 55:248–58.

Milne, L. J., Milne, M. J. 1950. Notes on the behavior of horned toads. *Am. Mid. Nat.* 44:720–41.

Minton, S. A., Jr., Minton, M. R. 1980. *Venomous Reptiles.* New York: Scribner's. 308 pp.

Mintzer, A. C. 1982. Copulatory behavior and mate selection in the harvester ant, *Pogonomyrmex californicus* (Hymenoptera: Formicidae). *Ann. Entomol. Soc. Am.* 75:323–26.

Mitchell, J. D., Pierce, W. D. 1912. The ants of Victoria County, Texas. *Proc. Entomol. Soc. Wash.* 14:67–76.

Montanucci, R. R. 1981. Habitat separation between *Phrynosoma douglassi* and *P. orbiculare* (Lacertilia: Iguanidae) in Mexico. *Copeia* 1981:147–53.

Morrill, W. L. 1975. An unusual predator of the Florida harvester ant. *J. Georgia Entomol. Soc.* 10:50–51.

Munger, J. C. 1984a. Long-term yield from harvester ant colonies: implications for horned lizard foraging strategy. *Ecology* 65:1077–86.

———. 1984b. Optimal foraging? Patch use by horned lizards (Iguanidae: *Phrynosoma*). *Am. Nat.* 123:654–80.

———. 1984c. Home ranges of horned lizards (*Phrynosoma*): circumscribed and exclusive? *Oecologia* 62:351–60.

Philpot, V. B., Smith, R. G. 1950. Neutralization of pit viper venom by king snake serum. *Proc. Soc. Exp. Biol. Med.* 74:521–23.

Pianka, E. R., Parker, W. S. 1975. Ecology of horned lizards: a review with special reference to *Phrynosoma platyrhinos. Copeia* 1975:141–62.

Pianka, E. R., Pianka, H. D. 1970. The ecology of *Moloch horridus* (Lacertilia: Agamidae) in western Australia. *Copeia* 1970:90–103.

Porter, S. D., Eastmond, D. A. 1982. *Euryopis coki* (Theridiidae), a spider that preys on *Pogonomyrmex* ants *J. Arachnol.* 10:275–77.

Porter, S. D., Jorgensen, C. D. 1981. Foragers of the harvester ant, *Pogonomyrmex owyheei:* a disposable caste? *Behav. Ecol. Sociobiol.* 9:247–56.

———. 1988. Longevity of harvester ant colonies in southern Idaho. J. Range Manag. 41:104–7.

Powell, G. L., Russell, A. P. 1985a. Growth and sexual size dimorphism in Alberta populations of the eastern short-horned lizard, *Phrynosoma douglassi brevirostre. Can. J. Zool.* 63:139–54.

———. 1985b. Field thermal ecology of the eastern short-horned lizard (*Phrynosoma douglassi brevirostre*) in southern Alberta. *Can. J. Zool.* 63: 228–38.

Rissing, S. W. 1981. Prey preferences in the desert horned lizard: influence of prey foraging method and aggressive behavior. *Ecology* 62:1031–40.

Rogers, L. E. 1974. Foraging activity of the western harvester ant on the shortgrass plains ecosystem. *Environ. Entomol.* 3:420–24.

Rogers, L. E., Lavigne, R. J. 1974. Environmental effects of western harvester ant in the shortgrass plains ecosystem. *Environ. Entomol.* 3:994–97.

Rogers, L. E., Lavigne, R., Miller, J. I. 1972. Bioenergetics of the western harvester ant in the shortgrass plains ecosystem. *Environ. Entomol.* 1:763–68.

Rosenfeld, S., Glass, S. 1940. The inhibiting effect of snake bloods upon the hemorrhagic action of viper venoms on mice. *Am. J. Med. Sci.* 199:482–86.

Schmidt, J. O. 1983. Hymenopteran envenomation. In *Urban Entomology: Interdisciplinary Perspectives.* Eds. G. W. Frankie and C. S. Koehler, 187–220. New York: Praeger. 493 pp.

———. 1986. Chemistry, pharmacology, and chemical ecology of ant venoms. In *Venoms of the Hymenoptera.* Ed. T. Piek, 425–508. London: Academic. 570 pp.

———. Hymenopteran venoms: striving toward the ultimate defense against vertebrates. In *Arthropod Defenses: Adaptive Mechanisms and Strategies of Prey and Predators.* Ed.

D. L. Evans and J. O. Schmidt. Albany, New York: State University of New York Press. (In press.)

Schmidt, J. O., Blum, M. S. 1978. A harvester ant venom: chemistry and pharmacology. *Science* 200:1064–66.

Schmidt, J. O., Blum, M. S.,, Overal, W. L. 1980. Comparative lethality of venoms from stinging Hymenoptera. *Toxicon* 18:469–74.

———. 1984. Hemolytic activities of stinging insect venoms. *Arch. Insect Biochem. Physiol.* 1:155–60.

———. 1986. Comparative enzymology of venoms from stinging Hymenoptera. *Toxicon* 24:907–21.

Schmidt, P. J., Sherbrooke, W. C., Schmidt, J. O. 1989. The detoxification of ant (*Pogonomyrmex*) venom by a blood factor in horned lizards (*Phrynosoma*). *Copeia* 1989:603–7.

Sharp, L. A., Barr, W. F. 1960. Preliminary investigations of harvester ants on southern Idaho rangelands. *J. Range Manag.* 13:131–34.

Sherbrooke, W. C. 1981. *Horned Lizards Unique Reptiles of Western North America.* Globe, Arizona: Southwest Parks and Monuments Assoc. 48 pp.

Spangler, H. G., Rettenmeyer, C. W. 1966. The function of the ammochaetae, or psammophores of harvester ants, *Pogonomyrmex* spp. *J. Kansas Entomol. Soc.* 39:739–45.

Stebbins, R. C. 1985. *A Field Guide to Western Reptiles and Amphibians.* 2d ed. Boston: Houghton Mifflin. 336 pp.

Straight, R., Glenn, J. L., Snyder, C. C. 1976. Antivenom activity of rattlesnake blood plasma. *Nature* 261:259–60.

Tanner, W. W., Krogh, J. E. 1973. Ecology of *Phrynosoma platyrhinos* at the Nevada test site, Nye County, Nevada. *Herpetologia* 29:327–42.

Tollestrup, K. 1981. The social behavior and displays of two species of horned lizards, *Phrynosoma platyrhinos* and *Phrynosoma coronatum*. *Herpetologia* 37:130–41.

Tomaszewski, E. K., Schaffer, H. E., Johnson, F. M. 1973. Isozyme genotype-environment associations in natural populations of the harvester ant, *Pogonomyrmex badius*. *Genetics* 75:405–21.

Turner, F. B., Medica, P. A. 1982. The distribution and abundance of the flat-tailed horned lizard (*Phrynosoma mcallii*). *Copeia* 1982:815–23.

Wheeler, W. M. 1910. *Ants Their Structure, Development and Behavior.* New York: Columbia University Press. 663 pp.

Wheeler, G. C., Wheeler, J. 1963. *The Ants of North Dakota.* Grand Forks, ND: University of North Dakota Press. 326 pp.

———. 1973. *Ants of Deep Canyon.* Riverside: University of California Press. 162 pp.

Whitford, W. G. 1978. Structure and seasonal activity of a Chihuahuan Desert ant community. *Insectes Soc.* 25:79–88.

Whitford, W. G., Bryant, M. 1979. Behavior of a predator and its prey: the horned lizard (*Phrynosoma cornutum*) and harvester ants (*Pogonomyrmex* spp.). *Ecology* 60:686–94.

Whitford, W. G., Ettershank, G. 1975. Factors affecting foraging activity in Chihuahuan Desert harvester ants. *Environ. Entomol.* 4:689–96.

Whitford, W. G., Johnson, P., Ramirez, J. 1976. Comparative ecology of the harvester ants *Pogonomyrmex barbatus* (F. Smith) and *Pogonomyrmex rugosus* (Emery). *Insectes Soc.* 23:117–32.

Willard, J. R., Crowell, H. H. 1965. Biological activities of the harvester ant, *Pogonomyrmex owyheei*, in central Oregon. *J. Econ. Entomol.* 58:484–89.

Winton, W. M. 1915. A preliminary note on the food habits and distribution of the Texas horned lizards. *Science* 41:797–98.

Wray, D. L. 1938. Notes on the southern harvester ant (*Pogonomyrmex badius* Latr.) in North Carolina. *Ann. Entomol. Soc. Am.* 31:196–201.

# 3

# THE NATURAL HISTORY AND ROLE OF SUBTERRANEAN TERMITES IN THE NORTHERN CHIHUAHUAN DESERT

William P. MacKay, John C. Zak,
and Walter G. Whitford

New Mexico State University
Las Cruces, New Mexico

## INTRODUCTION

*Gnathamitermes tubiformans* (Buckley) (Isoptera: Termitidae) is a subterranean termite that lives in diffuse nests of scattered chambers in the soil of the northern Chihuahuan Desert. Although most of the activity of *G. tubiformans* is below ground, during rainy seasons aboveground foraging may be common. Generally, however, there is little indication of their presence aboveground. *Amitermes wheeleri* (Desneux) also occurs in the area but is not as common as *G. tubiformans*, and its activity is restricted to below the soil surface. Because much of the termite activity in the Chihuahuan Desert occurs below ground, subterranean termites have proven to be difficult subjects for research, and what is known of their natural history is inferred from studies of their aboveground activity (Haverty and Nutting 1975; Johnson and Whitford 1975; La Fage, Haverty and Nutting, 1976). The research completed suggests that *G. tubiformans* is a keystone species in the functioning of the Chihuahuan Desert ecosystem (Whitford, Steinberger and Ettershank, 1982, Elkins et al. 1986).

In this chapter, we summarize what is known about *G. tubiformans* and include discussions on (1) population estimates, (2) diurnal and seasonal aboveground activity patterns, (3) aboveground gallery construction, (4) their importance in nitrogen cycling and the breakdown of organic matter, (5) interactions with microarthropods, (6) effects on soil infiltration rates, and (7) effects on plant communities.

53

## STUDY AREA

The majority of the information presented was obtained from studies conducted on the LTER (NSF–Long Term Ecological Research) Jornada site located 40 km north northeast of Las Cruces, Doña Ana County, New Mexico. The vegetation is sparse, consisting of spring- and summer-flowering annuals (for example, *Baileya multiradiata* Harv. and Gray, *Eriogonum trichopes* Torr., *Lepidium lasiocarpum* [Nutt.]), perennials (*Erioneuron pulchellum* Takeoka, *Zinnia grandiflora* Nutt., *Xanthocephalum sarothrae [Pursh]*) and a few shrubs (for example, *Larrea tridentata* [DC.] Cov.). The long-term average annual precipitation is 210 mm, 55% of which occurs during July–September as convectional storms. Summer maximum air temperatures average 40° C and winter air temperatures regularly fall below 0° C (Whitford et al. 1982).

## EXPERIMENTAL EXCLUSION OF TERMITES

In 1977, a factorial-designed experiment was initiated to assess the effects of termite removal on litter decomposition, nutrient cycling, and plant productivity (Elkins et al. 1986). The experimental design consisted of four blocks, each composed of five completely randomized treatment plots (30 x 40 m). Two plots of each block were treated with 10.3 kg/ha of the insecticide chlordane to eliminate termites. No active arthropods or nematodes were found in treated soils to a depth of 20 cm through the spring of 1978. By mid-fall, essentially all arthropods with the exception of termites had recolonized the upper few centimeters of soil (Elkins 1983; Whitford and Freckman, unpublished data). Treated soils on the Jornada have been constantly devoid of termites up to the present time.

## POPULATION ESTIMATES

Studies of subterrranean termites at the Jornada site were initiated as part of the US/IBP Desert Biome program utilizing techniques recommended by Dr. William Nutting, University of Arizona, Tucson. Based on La Fage, Nutting, and Haverty (1973), Johnson and Whitford (1975) established a series of eight grids, each consisting of 100 toilet paper rolls that were placed one meter apart on representative areas of the LTER watershed to obtain population estimates and to determine termite activity patterns. The rolls were placed over metal stakes with one end directly in contact with the soil surface. Termite activity was monitored by lifting the rolls and counting the numbers of foragers on the soil surface and in the rolls at two-hour intevals. No roll was handled more than once a day. The original rolls were removed and replaced in March 1973, after nine months exposure. Population estimates were continued during the 1973 growing season. We must emphasize that this method estimates only the number of foragers, thus underestimating the actual termite population.

Population estimates of some genera of termites can also be obtained using the territorial behavior of the animals. Colonies may be delineated by mixing termites from different rolls. If fighting occurs, one can conclude that the two groups of termites belong to different colonies (Schaefer and Whitford 1981). Once colonies have been delineated, the number of termites in a given area can be obtained by multiplying the average number of termites in a colony by the number of colonies. W.L. Nutting (personal communication) found that there were between 5,000–10,000 individuals in a *Gnathamitermes perplexus* colony. Even though conservative, these estimates using only foragers demonstrate the tremendous numbers and biomass of termites in the northern Chihuahuan Desert (Table 3.1). The biomass of termites is about 10 times that of the cattle that can be sustained on rangelands in this area, suggesting that cattle are not the most efficient processors of vegetation in this region. Given that our estimates are about 50% of those of Ueckert, Bodine, and Spears (1976) for *G. tubiformans* in a shortgrass prairie, the impact of *G. tubiformans* on the Chihuahuan Desert ecosystems may be considerable.

## ABOVEGROUND FORAGING PATTERNS

In 1982, the Jornada LTER group established a transect, from a playa basin to the base of Mt. Summerford, to study the spatial and temporal variability in primary production, decomposition, nutrient cycling, and surface termite activity along the watershed. The transect passes through a number of plant communities, ranging from the playa to a mesquite-covered playa fringe, a mixed basin bajada consisting of a number of species of com-

Table 3.1 Comparison of termite and cattle biomass in the northern Chihuahuan Desert

| Group | Density (numbers $\cdot$ ha$^{-1}$) | Mass (g $\cdot$ ha$^{-1}$) |
|---|---|---|
| Termites | $1.2 \times 10^7$ | 30,000 |
| Cattle | 0.009 | 3,125 |

mon desert annuals, a creosote shrub zone, a fluff grass zone, and a black grama grass area near the base of Mt. Summerford. The transect has stations every 30 m. At each station, four toilet paper rolls were wrapped with aluminum foil and placed over metal stakes (Fig. 3.1). One end of each roll was in contact with the soil surface. The rolls were checked once every two weeks for termite activity during the year.

Termites were very active in the fall of 1982 in most communities (Fig. 3.2). Activity peaked in mid-September–early October. By the end of November, termites were no longer active. Termite activity began again in March of the following year and increased into mid-summer. Again termites were not active after November. Several ecologists have reported

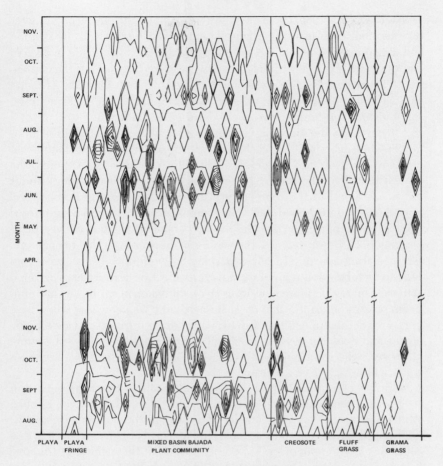

Figure 3.2. Spatial and temporal surface activity of sub-terranean termites feeding on rolls of toilet paper along a transect passing through several desert plant communities. The diamonds indicate activity levels with those composed of more lines representing higher activity.

that aboveground foraging in termites is exogenously controlled by soil temperature and moisture conditions (Kemp 1955; Smythe and Williams 1972; Haverty, LaFage, and Nutting 1974; Haverty and Nutting 1976; La Fage, Haverty, and Nutting 1976). The importance of these factors is not surprising, as the integument of subterranean termites is thin and deli-cate, and therefore the termites are susceptible to loss of body moisture through evaporation (Ueckert, Bodine, and Spears 1976).

MacKay et al. (1986) experimentally determined the effects of temperature and moisture on aboveground foraging of *G. tubiformans* by shading
and irrigating several plots. A grid of 96 depressions was made in each of
four plots and about 50 g of mixed litter were placed into each of the depressions. Eight depresssions were checked every 2 hours for up to 24 hours
and marked to exclude them from further examination. At the same time,
soil moisture and temperature were determined under the litter and at 5
and 10 cm below the soil surface. This experiment was repeated three times
in 1983 and once in 1984, each time with fresh litter. It was found that
only soil moisture at 5 cm depth affected termite activity. Although the
shaded plots had lower soil temperatures than the controls, the termites
did not respond to the temperature differences. Ueckert, Bodine, and
Spears (1976) determined that only when precipitation was above normal
was soil temperature the most important parameter afecting aboveground
foraging in *G. tubiformans*. Otherwise, soil moisture was the key parameter regulating activity. In our experiments, we found that at least from
May to October, soil temperature had no effect on termite aboveground
activity. Soil temperature may act as an on-off switch in spring and autumn.
From studies of termite activity at surface baits, we know that when temperatures of the upper 5 cm drop to near freezing, termite surface-feeding
ceases and does not resume until soil temperatures rise above freezing.
However, when soil temperatures are favorable, soil moisture regulates
activity in surface litter accumulations.

Whitford et al. (unpublished data) have found that there are persistent
long-term precipitation patterns in the northern Chihuahuan Desert,
although they are less predictable than those in the Sonoran Desert (R.
Nielson, personal communication). Rainfall usually begins in late July and
continues until October or November. Much of the rainfall in the area
falls during this time. MacKay et al. (1986) predicted that termites should
stop aboveground foraging when the soil moisture is less than −5.4 MPa.
Apparently, late-summer precipitation in the northern Chihuahuan Desert is the key factor which stimulates an increase in aboveground activity
of termites at this time.

In adddition to a seasonal change in activity, MacKay et al. (1986) found
that termites exhibit diurnal variation in surface activity (Fig. 3.3). During the summer, termites are most active aboveground during the late
afternoon, night, and early morning hours. During mid-day, activity ceases.
In late fall, the termites are active throughout the day.

Termite activity was also found to vary spatially along the LTER transect (Fig. 3.2). Termites were absent in the playa, possibly due to heavy
clay soils or to periodic flooding. Activity in the playa fringe was low,
although more dead wood (mesquite) is available there than anywhere on

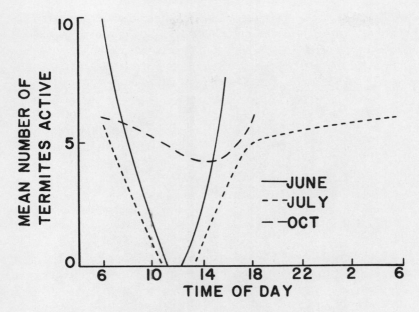

Figure 3.3.   Diurnal variation in aboveground activity of
*Gnathamitermes tubiformans*.

the transect (MacKay et al., unpublished). Apparently *G. tubiformans* does
not use mesquite wood (Johnson and Whitford 1975). The mixed basin
bajada demonstrated a lot of activity, the creosote zone slightly less. Activity was lower in the fluff grass and black grama grass areas, which have
coarse sandy and rocky soil.

## ABOVEGROUND GALLERY CONSTRUCTION

When soil is moist, *G. tubiformans* constructs mud galleries around dead
branches of several species of desert shrubs and surface litter (Fig. 3.4)
and around forbs and grasses (Whitford, Steinberger, and Ettershank 1982).
Each termite carries a single soil particle in its mandibles which it cements
into place during gallery construction. Galleries may protect termites from
desiccation, from predators, or from competitors.

Examination of termite galleries showed that longer gallery systems in
standing dead vegetation are more massive per unit length than those on
the soil surface (MacKay et al. 1985) (Fig. 3.5). Apparently the termites
construct taller gallery systems with greater structural strength. This factor,

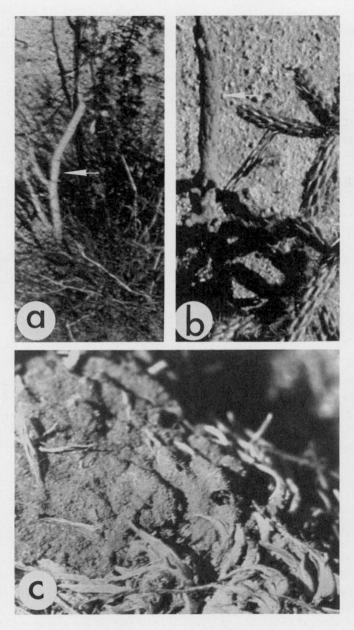

Figure 3.4.    Gallery system of *Gnathamitermes tubiformans* on standing dead wood of *a*, creosotebush; *b*, cholla; and *c*, on surface litter.

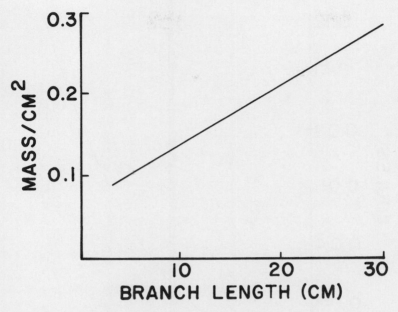

Figure 3.5.    Effect of mass/cm versus height of the gallery system of *G. tubiformans* (from MacKay et al. 1985).

in addition to the actual energetic costs of termites raising their loads and body mass to higher levels, make the costs of gallery construction increase rapidly after the first 10 cm (Fig. 3.6). Yet, termites often construct galleries a meter or more into the canopies of desert shrubs. Obviously, gallery construction is energetically very expensive.

Termites in the Chihuahuan Desert graze primarily on the outer surface of dead wood and remove the layer that is highest in nitrogen (Fig. 3.7). It appeared that the termites were investing large amounts of energy to harvest a very small mass of material. We hypothesized that the energetic cost of construction was actually greater than the energy the termites obtained from eating the wood, but that they continued this process to obtain resources relatively high in nitrogen. In other words, the important "currency" was not calories, but units of nitrogen.

MacKay et al. (1985) analyzed the energy content of the outer layer of wood that the termites removed and rejected the higher energetic cost hypothesis. They found that the amount of energy the termites received was very high, about six orders of magnitude greater than the energy invested in gallery construction. It was concluded that termites actually obtained a large return on the energy invested, in addition to obtaining a

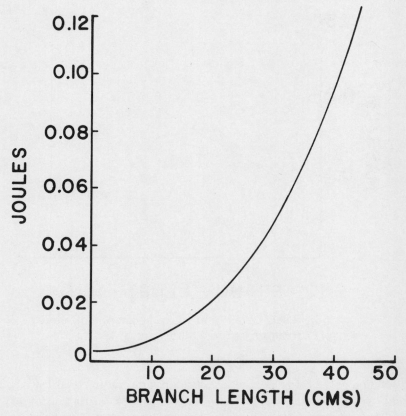

Figure 3.6.    Relationship between cost of construction of the gallery system of *G. tubiformans* and the height of standing dead branches (from MacKay et al. 1985).

food source relatively high in nitrogen. As certain processes are limited by nitrogen in the Chihuahuan Desert (Ettershank et al. 1978; MacKay et al. 1987; Whitford et al., unpublished), we assumed that termite populations would also be limited by nitrogen.

## TERMITES AND NITROGEN CYCLING

A significant fraction of the nitrogen turnover in the Chihuahuan Desert passes through termites and returns to the system by way of termite predators (Fig. 3.8). Nitrogen is also cycled back into the system from the aboveground galleries (Schaefer and Whitford 1981). The quantity of gal-

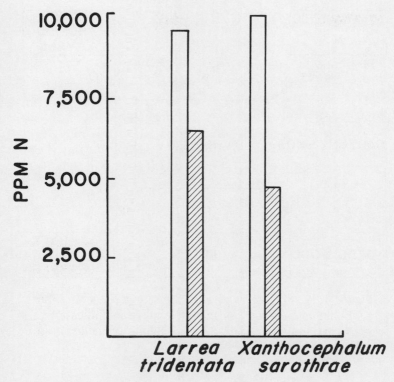

Figure 3.7.   Comparison of the nitrogen levels in ungrazed (open bars) and grazed wood (hatched bars) in creosote (*Larrea tridentata*) and snakeweed (*Xanthocephalum sarothrae*).

lery carton produced per year at the LTER study area ranged from 95 to $272 \ kg \cdot ha^{-1}$ over a three-year period (Whitford, Steinberger, and Ettershank 1982), which would account for nitrogen inputs of between 14 and $40 \ g \cdot ha^{-1}$ (Whitford et al. 1983).

Termites obtain nitrogen from a number of sources. The intestinal bacterial flora of termites are able to fix atmospheric nitrogen (Benemann 1973; Breznak et al. 1973; French, Turner, and Bradbury 1976; Schaefer and Whitford 1979, 1981; Preswich, Bentley, and Carpenter 1980; Prestwich and Bentley 1981, 1982). Schaefer and Whitford (1981) estimated that $66 \ g$ of nitrogen per year $\cdot ha^{-1}$ were fixed by the gut microflora of termites. Most of the nitrogen in termites, however, is obtained from the consumption of organic matter. Litter contributes the greatest amount, dead wood is second, and annuals and grasses are last (Fig. 3.8). In a recent study which examined the decomposition of roots of two Chihuahuan Des-

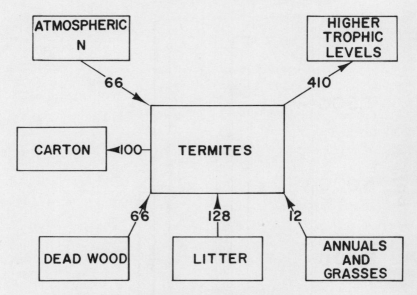

Figure 3.8. Role of termites in the nitrogen cycle in the Chihuahuan Desert ecosystem. The numbers indicate the grams of nitrogen transferred per year $\cdot$ ha$^{-1}$ (modified from Schaefer and Whitford 1981).

ert annuals, *Baileya multiradiata* and *Eriogonum trichopes*, Stinnet and Whitford (unpublished data) found that termites consumed a significant fraction of dead roots of these annuals. Although the amount of root standing crop consumed by termites has not been measured, the nitrogen contribution by roots into the termite subsystem could be large enough to account for the discrepancy between inputs and outputs in Figure 3.8.

Based on calculations by Schaefer and Whitford (1981), we have estimated that 879 g N $\cdot$ ha$^{-1}$ are incorporated into termite biomass per year. Of this, 510 g is recycled annually through carton production and predation. Predation accounts for 80% of the N flux through the termite subsystem.

Studies by Schaefer and Whitford (1981) and Parker et al. (1982) have indicated that subterranean termites may be an important nitrogen sink in the Chihuahuan Desert. Termites translocate large quantities of dead plant material into deep colony galleries. Nutrients in this material are thus not available to shallow-rooted plants. Termites are trophylactic feeders and also dispose of old or damaged individuals by cannibalism. Actual estimates of nitrogen content of soils with termites experimentally removed showed significantly higher nitrogen levels in the superficial soil layers (0–20 cm) (Parker et al. 1982).

## IMPORTANCE OF TERMITES IN THE BREAKDOWN OF ORGANIC MATTER

Termites have been shown to be very important in the breakdown of organic matter in a number of ecosystems (Ebert and Zedler 1984; Harmon et al. 1986). They are responsible for up to 100% of the mass loss from organic matter in the Chihuahuan Desert (Whitford, Steinberger, and Ettershank 1982) and can reduce the half-life of ocotillo wood in the Colorado Desert from 29 to 17 years (Ebert and Zedler 1984).

In a study where termites were eliminated from an area of the Chihuahuan Desert with the insecticide chlordane (Whitford, Steinberger, and Ettershank 1982), mass loss of fluff grass was highest in the plots with termites (Fig. 3.9a). After one year, about 50% of the mass was gone compared to about 20% in the termite-free plots (Silva, MacKay, and Whitford 1985). Whitford, Steinberger, and Ettershank (1982) reported that pieces of yucca stalk lost over 20% of their mass in plots with termites during a 30-month experiment while stalks in plots without termites lost only about 10% (Fig. 3.9b). In a recent study that examined the effect of termites on mass loss of creosote wood, termite-attacked wood lost significantly more mass over a one-year period than nongrazed wood (Fig. 3.9c). In a two-year study that examined the role of termites in the decomposition of creosotebush litter, MacKay et al. (unpublished) found that termites did not significantly affect mass loss (Fig. 3.10). Fowler and Whitford (1980) had reported earlier that *G. tubiformans* does not readily attack creosotebush leaf litter. Later observations and data demonstrated that termites would graze creosotebush leaves, but only when other material was not available.

*Gnathamitermes tubiformans* is especially active in attacking standing dead and surface wood and certain types of litter in the northern Chihuahuan Desert. Occasionally, they will attack an injured shrub. Leaf litter that is buried by either wind-blown sand or by rodent activity is not attacked by termites (Santos 1979; Ettershank, Ettershank, and Whitford 1980). Termites will graze buried wood and dead roots (Zak, unpublished data).

Much of the Chihuahuan Desert is currently grazed by cattle. In such areas, the feces are usually dry before the dung macro- and microfauna (that is, scarab beetles, dipteran larvae) are able to colonize the substrate. Long after such feces are air dried, they continue to be attacked by termites (Whitford, Steinberger, and Ettershank 1982). In plots with termites, mass loss from cattle dung was low until the fall rains, at which time almost 50% of the original mass was lost (Fig. 3.11). Without termites, mass loss

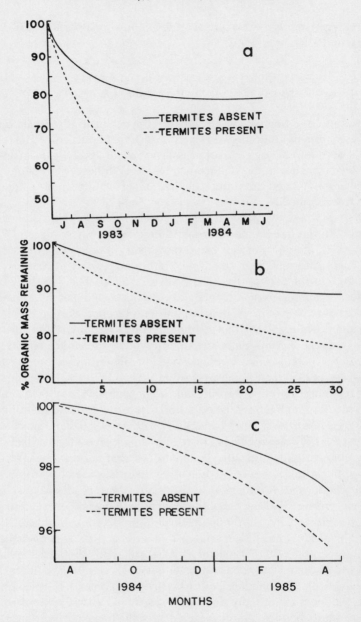

Figure 3.9.    Mass loss of organic matter from plots with and without termites, including *a*, fluff grass (*Erioneuron pulchellum* (data from Silva et al. 1985); *b*, yucca (*Yucca elata*) stalks; and *c*, creosotebush (*Larrea tridentata*) wood.

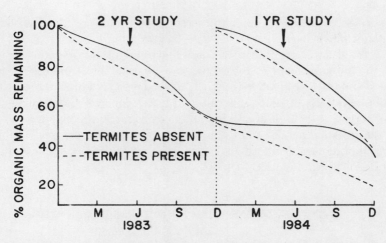

Figure 3.10. Mass loss from creosote leaf litter in plots with and without termites.

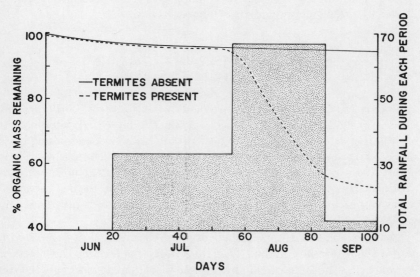

Figure 3.11. Mass loss from cattle dung in plots with and without termites. Total rainfall is indicated by the stippled region (from Whitford et al. 1982).

was negligible. During the rainy season cattle feces are literally riddled with termite galleries.

Termite activity appears to be controlled by abiotic factors acting directly on the individual and by those abiotic factors that affect the rate of dead wood and litter production (Fig. 3.12). Dead wood is added to the system from the effects of wind, snowfall, and insect damage. Litter falls to the soil surface as a result of drought and/or nutrient stress, changes in temperature, wind action, and the browsing of mammals, especially rabbits (Steinberger and Whitford 1983). Temperature extremes and lack of precipitation also kill roots.

## INTERACTIONS WITH MICROARTHROPODS

Populations of soil microarthropods (mites, Collembola, Psocoptera) were compared in fluff grass litter in plots with and without termites (S. Silva, W. MacKay & W. Whitford, unpublished data). Since mites, Collembola, Psocoptera, and termites feed either directly or indirectly on the litter, competition for this resource could be expected to determine population numbers. Plots from which the termites were removed had consistently higher densities of microarthropods (Fig. 3.13). Removal of the termites would have lowered competitive interactions which could have resulted in the observed higher numbers of microathropods.

## EFFECT OF SUBTERRANEAN TERMITES ON SOIL INFILTRATION RATES

Bodine and Ueckert (1975) determined that exclusion of G. tubiformans from a shortgrass prairie in west Texas resulted in increased water infiltration in this habitat. The mulching effect of the slowly decomposing grass not consumed by termites enhanced soil-water status. In contrast, Elkins et al. (1986) found that exclusion of G. tubiformans in the northern Chihuahuan Desert decreased water infiltration rates due to the absence of gallery tunnels which would normally allow the water to rapidly enter the soil (Fig. 3.14).

Whitford and Ward (unpublished) established run-off plots on areas with and without termites on the LTER study area to determine the effects of termites on water infiltration rates. These plots (2 m square) directed the sheet flow onto an apron which in turn dumped water into a PVC sewer pipe draining into a barrel (Fig. 3.15). Water was collected and measured after natural rainfall and artificial irrigation of the plots. Plots without ter-

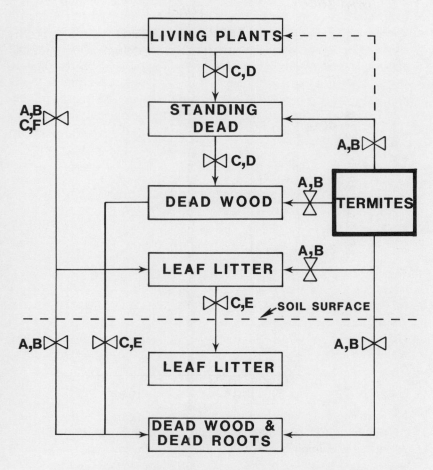

A-Rainfall (timing, intensity, spacing)

B-Temperature (diurnal, seasonal)

C-Wind

D-Snowfall, Insect Damage

E-Rodent Excavation

F-Browsing, especially by rabbits

Figure 3.12. A schematic representation of the role of termites in the breakdown of organic matter.

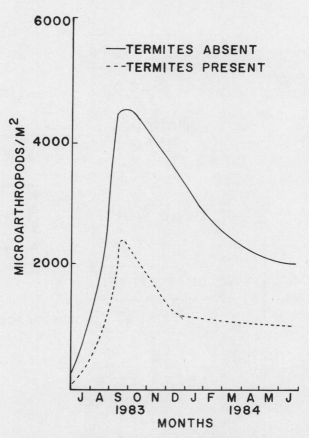

Figure 3.13.    Populations of soil microarthropods in fluff grass litter in plots with and without termites.

mites began to have sheet-flow within 5 minutes of initiation of artificial irrigation; plots with termites began to "run" only after 15 minutes (Fig. 3.16). The total volume of run-off was much greater in plots without termites.

## EFFECT OF SUBTERRANEAN TERMITES ON DESERT PLANT COMMUNITIES

The effects of termites, water, and nitrogen on the composition and flowering phenology of the Chihuahuan Desert plant community was examined in a study by Gutierrez (1984). Changes in dominance of annual plant

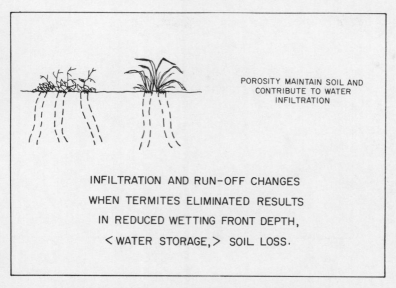

POROSITY MAINTAIN SOIL AND
CONTRIBUTE TO WATER
INFILTRATION

INFILTRATION AND RUN-OFF CHANGES
WHEN TERMITES ELIMINATED RESULTS
IN REDUCED WETTING FRONT DEPTH,
< WATER STORAGE, > SOIL LOSS.

Figure 3.14.   Gallery system of termites which leads to greater water infiltration and less run-off.

Figure 3.15.   Run-off plot in areas with and without termites.

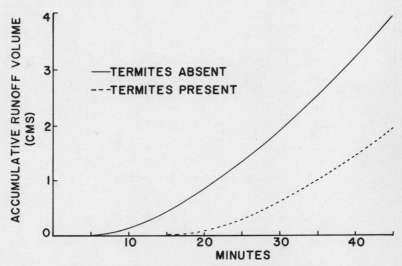

Figure 3.16.    Accumulative run-off volumes in areas with and without termites.

species were obtained within three years after termite removal. While some species, such as *Eriastrum diffusum*, were not affected by the treatments (Fig. 3.17), others (for example, *Baileya multiradiata, Descurainea pinnata, Eriogonum rotundifolium,* and *Lepidium lasiocarpum*) became more common in plots with termites removed. The phenologies of some species were also reduced when the termites were eliminated. Two species showing this pattern include *Eriogonum tricopes* and *Tidestromia lanuginosa.*) Fluff grass *(Erioneuron pulchellum)* virtually disappeared from plots without termites by the fourth year following eradication.

The addition of water and/or nitrogen resulted in occurrence of four plant species, *B. multiradiata, D. pinnata, E. rotundifolium,* and *L. lasiocarpum,* which were not present on plots with termites only (Fig. 3.17). These species were found on all treatments where termites had been removed. These data indicated that termite activity had a negative effect on the presence of these plants. The removal of termites and the addition of water and/or nitrogen also resulted in changes in the lengths of time these annuals were present in the plots and the time of first occurrence. For example, *B. multiradiata* first occurred in August on the termite plus water plots and was present in these plots until October of the following year. In contrast, *B. multiradiata* first occurred in April on the termite plus nitrogen plots and was present only through October. These results indicate that termites do have an effect on the composition and dynamics of desert plant com-

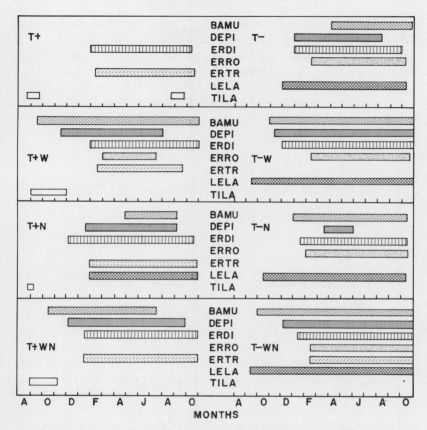

Figure 3.17.   Comparison of the effects of termites, water, and/or nitrogen on the phenology of Chihuahuan desert plant community. BAMU = *Baileya multiradiata*, DEPI = *Descurainea pinnata*, ERDI = *Eriastrum diffusum*, ERRO = *Eriogonum rotundifolium*, ERTR = *Eriogonum tricopes*, LELA = *Lepidium lasiocarpum*, and TILA = *Tidestromia lanuginosa* (from Gutierrez 1984).

munities. The interactions among termites, water, and nitrogen on plant growth appear to be complex and depend on the plant species examined.

## CONCLUSIONS

We have shown that *Gnathamitermes tubiformans* plays a keystone role in the functioning of the northern Chihuahuan Desert ecosystem. Subterranean termites are the most important organisms involved in the breakdown of organic matter on the soil surface, including livestock dung, yucca inflorescences, dead leaves, and annual plants and dead grasses (Fig. 3.18). They play an important role in nitrogen cycling in this system through their consumption of dead plant material, fixation of atmospheric nitrogen by gut symbionts, and production of nitrogen-enriched gallery carton. By influencing the infiltration rate of rainfall, termites have a major effect on

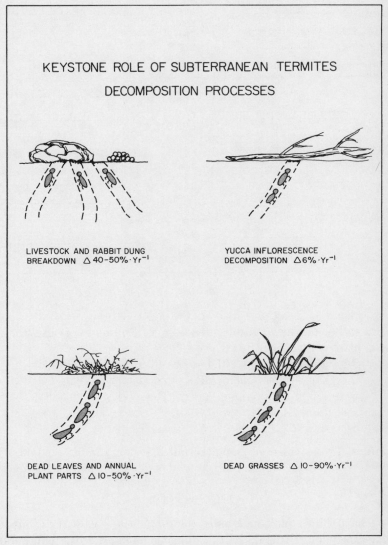

Figure 3.18.   The keystone role of subterranean termites in the northern Chihuahuan Desert.

the water status of the soil. The interactions among termites, nitrogen availability, and soil-water status can have significant effects on the composition and phenology of the desert plant community.

Although termites consume only dead organic matter, they have been characterized as competing with cattle (Bodine and Ueckert 1975; Spears, Ueckert, and Whigham 1975; Schaefer and Whitford 1981), and insecticide control measures have been suggested. Considering the importance of termites in nutrient cycling, water infiltration, and subsequent plant growth, treatment of rangelands by insecticides would do much more harm than good.

## ACKNOWLEDGMENTS

The authors wish to thank the numerous people who have been involved in the various termite projects at the Jornada site over several years. Special thanks go to Dr. Marsha Conley for seasonal activity data and Dr. Ron Nielson for plotting the data on spatial termite activity—Jill Eash prepared the figures. Brenda Massad and Elizabeth Stevens typed the manuscript. The research was supported by the International Biological Program, and NSF grants numbers BSR 821539 and BSR 8406708.

## REFERENCES

Benemann, J. R. 1973. Nitrogen fixation in termites. *Science* 181:164–65.

Bodine, M. C., Ueckert, D. M. 1975. Effect of desert termites on herbage and litter in a shortgrass ecosystem in west Texas. *J. Range Manag.* 28:353–58.

Breznak, J. A., Brill, W. J., Mertins, J. W., Coppel, H. C. 1973. Nitrogen fixation in termites. *Nature* 244:577–80.

Ebert, T. A., Zedler, P. H. 1984. Decomposition of ocotillo (*Fouquieria splendens*) wood in the Colorado Desert of California. *Am. Mid. Nat.* 111:143–47.

Elkins, N. Z. 1983. Potential mediation by desert subterranean termites in infiltration, runoff, and erosional soil loss on a desert watershed. Ph.D. dissertation, New Mexico State Univ., Las Cruces. 137 pp.

Elkins, N. Z., Sabol, G. V. Ward, T. J., Whitford, W. G. 1986. The influence of subterranean termites on the hydrological characteristics of a Chihuahuan Desert ecosystem. *Oecologia* 68:521–28.

Ettershank, G., Ettershank, J. A., Bryant, M., Whitford, W. G. 1978. Effects of nitrogen fertilization on primary production in a Chihuahuan Desert ecosystem. *J. Arid Environ.* 1:135–39.

Ettershank, G., Ettershank, J. A., Whitford, W. G. 1980. Location of food sources by subterranean termites. *Environ. Entomol.* 9:645–48.

Fowler, H., Whitford, W. G. 1980. Termites, microarthropods and the decomposition of senescent and fresh creosotebush (*Larrea tridentata*) leaf litter. *J. Arid Environ.* 3:63–68.

French, J. R., Turner, G. L., Bradbury, J. F. 1976. Nitrogen fixation by bacteria from the hindguts of termites. *J. Gen. Microbiol.* 95:202–7.

Gutierrez, J. R. 1984. Ephemeral plant responses to termites, water and nitrogen in a Chihuahuan desert. Ph.D. dissertation. New Mexico State Univ., Las Cruces. 102 pp.

Harmon, M. E., Franklin, J. F., Swanson, F. T., Sollins, P., Gregory, S. V., Lattin, J. D., Anderson, N. H., Cline, S. P., Aumen, N. G., Sedill, J. R., Lienkaemper, G. W., Cromack, K., Jr., Cummins, K. W. 1986. Ecology of coarse woody debris in temperate ecosystems. In *Advances in Ecological Research*. Vol. 15, 133–302. London: Academic Press.

Haverty, M. I., La Fage, J. P., Nutting, W. L. 1974. Seasonal activity and environmental control of foraging of the subterrranean termite *Heterotermes aureus* (Snyder) in a desert grassland. *Life Sci.* 15:1091–1101.

Haverty, M. I., Nutting, W. L. 1975. Density, dispersion and composition of desert termite foraging populations and their relationship to superficial dead wood. *Environ Entomol.* 4:480–86.

——. 1976. Environmental factors affecting the geographical distribution of two ecologically equivalent termite species in Arizona. *Am. Mid. Nat.* 95:20–27.

Johnson, K. A., Whitford, W. G. 1975. Foraging ecology and relative importance of subterranean termites in Chihuahuan Desert ecosystems. *Environ. Entomol.* 4:66–70.

Kemp, P. B. 1955. The termites of northeastern Tanganyika: their distribution and biology. *Bull. Entomol. Res.* 46:113–35.

La Fage, J. P., Nutting, W. L. Haverty, M. I. 1973. Desert subterranean termites: a method for studying foraging behavior. *Environ. Entomol.* 2:954–56.

La Fage, J. P., Haverty, M. I., Nutting, W. C. 1976. Environmental factors correlated with the foraging behavior of a desert subterranean termite *Gnathamitermes perplexus* (Banks) (Isoptera: Termitidae). *Sociobiology* 2:155–69.

MacKay, W. P., Blizzard, J. H., Miller, J. J., Whitford, W. G. 1985. An analysis of above ground gallery construction by the subterranean termite *Gnathamitermes tubiformans* (Isoptera: Termitidae). *Environ. Entomol.* 14:470–74.

MacKay, W. P., Fisher, F. M., Silva, S., Whitford, W. G. 1987. The effects of nitrogen, water and sulfur amendments on surface litter decomposition in the Chihuahuan Desert. *J. Arid Environ.* 12:223–32.

MacKay, W. P., Silva, S., Lightfoot, D. C., Pagani, M. I., Whitford, W. G. 1986. The effect of increased soil moisture and reduced soil temperature on a desert soil arthropod community. *Am. Mid. Nat.* 116:45–56.

Parker, L. W., Fowler, H. G., Ettershank, G., Whitford, W. G. 1982. The effects of subterranean termite removal on desert soil nitrogen and ephemeral flora. *J. Arid Environ.* 5:53–59.

Prestwich, G. D., Bentley, B. L. 1981. Nitrogen fixation by intact colonies of *Nasutitermes corniger*. *Oecologia* 49:249–51.

——. 1982. Ethylene production by the fungus comb of macrotermitines (Isoptera: Termitidae): a caveat for the use of the acetylene reduction assay for nitrogenase activity. *Sociobiology* 7:145–52.

Prestwich, G. D., Bentley, B. L., Carpenter, E. J. 1980. Nitrogen sources for neotropical nasute termites: fixation and selective foraging. *Oecologia* 46:397–401.

Santos, P. F. 1979. The role of microarthropods and nematodes in litter decomposition in a Chihuahuan Desert ecosystem. Ph.D. dissertation. New Mexico State Univ., Las Cruces. 82 pp.

Schaefer, D. A., Whitford, W. G. 1979. Nitrogen fixation in desert termites. *Bull. Ecol. Soc. Amer.* 60:128.

——. 1981. Nutrient cycling by the subterranean termite *Gnathamitermes tubiformans* in a Chihuahuan Desert ecosystem. *Oecologia* 58:277–83.

Silva, S., MacKay, W. P., Whitford, W. G. 1985. The relative contributions of termites and microarthropods to fluff grass litter disappearance in the Chihuahuan Desert. *Oecologia* 67:31–34.

Smythe, R. V., Williams, L. H. 1972. Feeding and survival of two subterranean termite species at constant temperatures. *Ann. Entomol. Soc. Amer.* 65:226–29.

Spears, B. M., Ueckert, D. N., Whigham, T. L. 1975. Desert termite control in short-grass prairie: effect on soil physical properties. *Environ. Entomol.* 4:899–904.

Steinberger, Y., Whitford, W. G. 1983. The contributions of shrub pruning by jackrabbits to litter input in a Chihuahuan Desert ecosystem. *J. Arid Environ.* 6:183–87.

Ueckert, D. N., Bodine, M. C., Spears, B. M. 1976. Population density and biomass of the desert termite *Gnathamitermes tubiformans* (Isoptera: Termitidae) in a short grass prairie: relationship to temperature and moisture. *Ecology* 57:1273–80.

Whitford, W. G., Freckman, D. W., Parker, L. W., Schaefer, D., Santos, P. F., Steinberger, Y. 1983. The contributions of soil fauna to nutrient cycles in desert systems. In *New Trends in Soil Biology*. Eds: Lebrun, P., Andre, H., De Medts, A., Gregoire-Wibo, C., Wanthy, G., 49–59. Ottignies-Louvain-la Nueve, Belgium: Dien-Brichard Press, 709 pp.

Whitford, W. G., Repass, R., Parker, L., Elkins, N. 1982. Effects of initial litter accumulation and climate on litter disappearance in a desert ecosystem. *Am. Mid. Nat.* 108:105–10.

Whitford, W. G., Steinberger, Y., Ettershank, G. 1982. Contributions of subterranean termites to the "economy" of Chihuahuan Desert ecosystems. *Oecologia* 55:298–302.

# 4

# FORAGING ECOLOGY OF SUBTERRANEAN TERMITES IN THE SONORAN DESERT

Susan C. Jones

USDA—FS Southern Forest Experiment Station
Gulfport, Mississippi

and

William L. Nutting

University of Arizona
Tucson, Arizona

## INTRODUCTION

Subterranean termites are of considerable importance from both an ecological and an economic perspective. Their cryptic nature, however, hinders in-depth studies of their foraging ecology. This chapter reviews available data, including current research by the authors,* on the foraging ecology of subterranean termites in the Sonoran Desert. Particular emphasis is given to food resources and preferences; abiotic and biotic factors that influence foraging activity; size and spatial patterns of territories; numbers and caste composition of foraging parties; and foraging behavior.

### The Sonoran Desert

The North American Desert is divided into four areas, of which the Sonoran Desert is the most species rich. The boundaries are defined by characteristic plants and animals, typically with emphasis on the former.

*S. C. Jones, Ph.D. dissertation (1987) at the University of Arizona, W. L. Nutting, major adviser.

A brief characterization of the physical features, flora, and termite fauna of the Sonoran Desert is given to provide background for the discussion of subterranean termite foraging ecology.

THE PHYSICAL FEATURES. The Sonoran Desert occupies about 310,000 km$^2$ and extends from southeastern California and southwestern Arizona into Mexico through the lowlands of Sonora to the Rio Yaqui and throughout Baja California, except for high mountains in the northwest and along the lower third of the peninsula (Fig. 4.1). Elevation ranges from approximately 1,040 m in eastern Arizona and northern Sonora, to sea level on the coasts of Sonora and Baja California, to below sea level in the vicinity of the Salton Sea in southern California. The Colorado is the only permanent river in the entire region today. Various aspects of the Sonoran Desert have been reviewed by Shreve (1964), McGinnies, Goldman, and Paylore (1968), and Turner and Brown (1982).

A fairly uniform continental climate prevails, with the temperatures ranging from some of the highest recorded for North America (53°C at Parker and Fort Mohave on the Colorado River) to occasionally heavy frosts in the northern and eastern sections. Annual rainfall generally increases in amount from west to east; less than 125 mm falls in the lower Colorado Valley and much of Baja California, with slightly more than 375 mm in eastern Arizona and Sonora. The seasonal distribution of precipitation also varies, with the extreme western areas receiving virtually all of their moisture from December to March. Frontal storms bring widespread gentle rains during the winter months. Going eastward, one sees the pattern shift so that the eastern borders of the desert receive a major allotment of rainfall from scattered, violent convectional storms during a well-defined summer season from July to September (Sellers 1960).

Fine-textured alluvial soils cover the plains, with gravel and bare rock around the base of the hills and mountains and thinning soils on the steeper slopes. Little humus accumulates in these soils, and vegetation is sparse. Some soils are underlain by caliche (a calcareous hardpan). In contrast with the deserts of Africa and Asia, sandy areas are uncommon. Beds of lava, some covering many square kilometers, are common.

THE FLORA. The flora of the Sonoran Desert is derived from subtropical elements to the south. The present distribution is very recent, dating back only 8,000 or 9,000 years, when drought conditions forced the retreat of the then existing woodlands (Axelrod 1979).

Vegetational patterns vary and interdigitate, depending upon soils, exposure, and elevation. The vegetation is generally sparse with open stretches of soil or rock between the plants. The creosote bush (*Larrea tridentata* [DC.] Coville) is the most widely distributed plant, with nearly pure stands covering extensive areas of the plains and lower bajadas. The irregular topog-

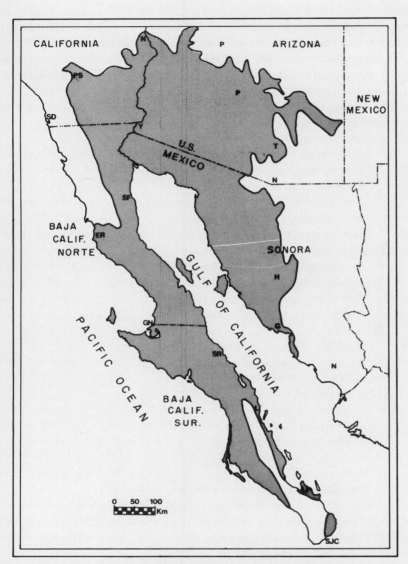

Figure 4.1.   Map with shaded area denoting the Sonoran
Desert. Initials are first letter of important cities.

raphy generally supports mixed stands of large shrubs, small trees, winter and summer annuals, and a variety of succulents. While many of the plants are thorny, there are probably as many that are not. Cacti are a most striking element, ranging from small pincushion types to large treelike forms. Various riparian associations occur along the larger streams and washes, such as mesquite (*Prosopis* spp.) bosques and woodlands of widely scattered cottonwoods (*Populus* sp.), willows (*Salix* spp.), sycamores (*Platanus* sp.), and hackberries (*Celtis* spp.).

THE TERMITE FAUNA.    Four families and 20 species are known from the Sonoran Desert:

Kalotermitidae
   *\*Pterotermes occidentis* (Walker)
   *\*Incisitermes banksi* (Snyder)
   *I. minor* (Hagen)
   *I. seeversi* (Snyder and Emerson)
   *Marginitermes hubbardi* (Banks)
   *\*Paraneotermes simplicicornis* (Banks)
Hodotermitidae
   *Zootermopsis laticeps* (Banks)
Rhinotermitidae
   *\*Heterotermes aureus* (Snyder)
   *Reticulitermes tibialis* Banks
Termitidae
   *Hoplotermes amplus* Light
   *Amitermes coachellae* Light
   *\*A. emersoni* Light
   *\*A. minimus* Light
   *\*A. pallidus* Light
   *A. parvulus* Light
   *\*A. silvestrianus* Light
   *A. snyderi* Light
   *\*A. wheeleri* (Desneux)
   *\*Gnathamitermes perplexus* (Banks)
   *\*Tenuirostritermes tenuirostris* (Desneux)

Starred (*) species occur on the Santa Rita Experimental Range, and biological details of the most abundant species are provided in the section where we discuss the study site.

According to Emerson (1955), Sonoran Desert termites (except *R. tibialis*) have their closest affinities with genera and species of the Neotropical Region. They generally avoid the extremes of temperature and drought by nesting in the ground and foraging on buried wood or within earthen shelters when in exposed situations.

*Pterotermes, Marginitermes,* and *Paraneotermes* are monotypic genera endemic to northwestern Mexico and the southwestern United States. The genus *Incisitermes* contains 23 species that are found in the Papuan, Indo-Malayan, Neotropical, and Nearctic regions, including 2 (*I. banksi* and *I. minor*) in the southwestern United States and 1 (*I. seeversi*) that is limited in the Sonoran Desert to the southern part of Baja California. *Heterotermes* has a semirelict worldwide distribution with several species in the neo-tropics and a single species (*H. aureus*) adapted to the arid conditions of the Sonoran Desert. *Reticulitermes* is a Holarctic genus, with *R. tibialis* ranging widely over the western United States, including the Sonoran Desert. Here it is apparently restricted to urban and riparian situations where suitable moisture and temperature conditions prevail; otherwise it is replaced by *Heterotermes aureus,* its ecological equivalent (Haverty and Nutting 1976). *Hoplotermes,* one of the least specialized of the termitids, is a monotypic Mexican genus with *H. amplus* found just within the bor-ders of the Sonoran Desert on the southern plains of Sonora. While *Amitermes* is a cosmopolitan, primarily tropical genus, at least eight spe-cies are found in the Sonoran Desert and adjacent semiarid areas. These species may well have evolved from Neotropical stock as they moved north-ward with the desertification of northwestern Mexico and the southwest-ern United States. *Gnathamitermes,* probably an offshoot of *Amitermes,* is another specialized genus endemic to western Mexico and the Ameri-can southwest. *Gnathamitermes perplexus* is very common in the Sonoran Desert and in adjacent semiarid areas. *Tenuirostritermes* is a small genus of four species that primarily are found in Central America, with *T. cinereus* (Buckley) extending into the Chihuahuan Desert and *T. tenuirostris* extend-ing into the Sonoran Desert and adjacent areas. These are the only Nearctic species of termites that have nasutiform soldiers.

## The Study Site

The Santa Rita Experimental Range, managed by the USDA Forest Ser-vice, is located about 40 km south of Tucson on the northwestern bajada of the Santa Rita Mountains. Since 1971 the area has been the site for most of the research on Sonoran Desert termite foraging ecology.

*THE PHYSICAL FEATURES.* The elevation at the study site is about 950 m, with a yearly rainfall average of 330 mm that is equally divided between summer and winter rainy seasons. Air temperatures range from around 40°C in summer to below 0°C in winter. In summer, the soil sur-face may reach 60°C during midday. The actual study site is on a slope of less than 3% and consists of Sonoita sandy loam that is formed from outwash alluvium. The soil is well drained between washes and is neutral (pH 6.8) at the surface to mildly alkaline (pH 7.8) at a depth of about 1.1 m (Chamberlin and Havens 1970).

THE FLORA.   The area is characterized as a shrub-invaded desert grassland, with cacti and small shrubs and trees scattered among the grasses. Common grasses include three-awn (*Aristida* spp.), grama (*Bouteloua* spp.), and Arizona cottontop (*Trichachne californica* [Benth.] Chase). Burro-weed (*Aplopappus tenuisectus* [Greene] Blake) dominates the shrub layer, while prickly pear and cholla (*Opuntia* spp.) are the prevalent cacti, and blue palo-verde (*Cercidium floridum* Benth.) is the dominant tree. Velvet mesquite (*Prosopis juliflora* var. *velutina* Woot. [Sarg.]) and catclaw acacia (*Acacia Greggii* Gray) also have invaded the area since the habitat has been disturbed by heavy grazing.

THE SUBTERRANEAN TERMITE FAUNA.   Subterranean termites live in more or less diffuse nests of scattered chambers in the soil with no aboveground mounds and few indications of the termites' presence. Nine subterranean species have been found on the Santa Rita Experimental Range. The most common species are *Paraneotermes simplicicornis*, *Heterotermes aureus*, and *G. perplexus*. *Amitermes* spp., primarily *A. minimus* and *A. wheeleri*, and *T. tenuirostris* are somewhat less common. *Amitermes emersoni*, *A. pallidus*, and *A. silvestrianus* also have been reported from the site. Some of the latter species probably are fairly common but are not readily detected by the current sampling techniques, which primarily are designed to detect surface populations. Several species are readily distinguished by characteristics of the soldier head and mouthparts (Fig. 4.2), as well as by size, shape, and color of the workers. Characteristic workings and damage to cellulosic material also help to identify species in the field.

*Paraneotermes simplicicornis* technically belongs to the family Kalotermitidae, or drywood termites. Nonetheless, behaviorally it is subterranean in its habits since it builds its nest and galleries in the soil and feeds only upon moist wood such as roots, stumps, and buried wood. Hence, this species is called "the desert damp-wood termite." It inhabits semiarid or desert country from southeastern California, southern Nevada, Arizona, and south central Texas, into northwestern Mexico, including Baja California. It is a minor pest that severs shrubs and young trees near ground level and occasionally attacks posts, poles, and buildings (Light 1937).

*Heterotermes aureus*, the desert subterranean termite, is the most common of the subterranean species in the Sonoran Desert below about 1,220 m. It occurs in the desert areas of southeastern California; southwestern Arizona; and Sonora, Sinaloa, and Baja California in Mexico. Haverty and

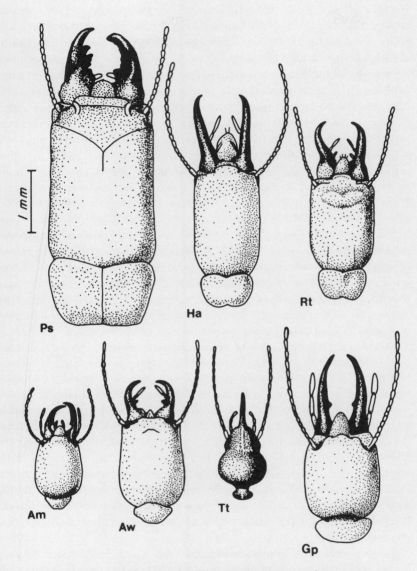

Figure 4.2.    Soldier heads of the most common subterranean termite species in the Sonoran Desert: *Ps, Paraneotermes simplicicornis; Ha, Heterotermes aureus; Rt, Reticulitermes tibialis; Am, Amitermes minimus; Aw, A. wheeleri; Tt, Tenuirostritermes tenuirostris*; and *Gp, Gnathamitermes perplexus*.

Nutting (1976) suggest that temperature and precipitation are inseparable factors influencing its distribution. However, it is capable of inhabiting some of the hottest and driest desert areas of Arizona because it can tolerate high temperatures and desiccation (Collins 1969) and its distribution appears to be limited by low rather than high temperatures (Haverty and Nutting 1976). It is extremely destructive and causes considerable damage to poles, posts, and wooden structures, from floor to rafters. Pickens and Light (1934) suggest that *H. aureus* would be among the most economically significant termite species in the United States, if it were not for its limited distribution.

*Gnathamitermes perplexus*, the tube-building desert termite, is found in southern California, southern Nevada, southwestern Arizona, northern Mexico, and extreme western Texas. It is very common at elevations below about 1,830 m (Nutting, unpublished data). It has a reputation as a pest primarily because of its building behavior, which is characterized by extensive aboveground earthen workings. Irregular tubes and broad earthen encrustations on cow chips, tree trunks, fences, lawns, and plant debris are most often the work of this termite. Because its feeding is confined to superficial layers of bark, dead wood, and fine, dry plant material, damage is usually negligible. Its habit of feeding upon wood from the outside is different from that of most subterranean termites.

Members of the genus *Amitermes* considered here are largely restricted to the deserts and semiarid regions and therefore are designated "desert termites." Two of the common species, *A. wheeleri* and *A. minimus*, are widely distributed, occurring in California, Nevada, Arizona, and southwestern Texas. *Amitermes wheeleri* also is widely distributed throughout the central plateau of Mexico (Nutting 1969a). Except for the biological and ecological notes included with the original descriptions (Light 1930a, 1930b, 1931, 1932), little has been published on the Nearctic members of the genus. This may be attributed to their extremely cryptic habits and occurrence in sparsely populated regions (Nutting 1969a). *Amitermes wheeleri* and *A. minimus* are of moderate economic importance because they penetrate sound wood, occasionally damaging poles and fence posts.

*Tenuirostritermes tenuirostris* ranges from southern Mexico and perhaps Guatemala (Snyder 1949) into southeastern Arizona. It is generally found in mountainous areas at elevations from 800 to 2,000 m, often under surface rocks. Its rapid erratic movements, dark color, and small size may cause it to be mistaken for one of the many smaller species of ants in the same habitat. While it is not known to be a pest, this species does harvest some living vegetation, and its abundance in agricultural areas makes it a potential crop pest (Nutting 1970a).

# FOOD RESOURCES

Termites probably owe their success to an early selection of cellulose as their basic energy source, for it is the most abundant of the continuously cycled organic materials in the biosphere. Termites are considered to be both primary consumers and decomposers of many different forms of cellulose, thus acting as "microruminants." This resource is shared with a variety of soil invertebrates fungi, and microorganisms. The flora of a region thus provides the basic food of its termite fauna. There are probably very few plants in the Sonoran Desert that are not eventually attacked by one or more members of the subterranean termite fauna.

## Form of Plant Material

Wood (1978) thoroughly reviewed the food and feeding habits of termites worldwide and classified the many plant materials that constitute their diet, emphasizing trophic level. These include living vegetation of all sorts, either aerial or subterranean; dead vegetation, either standing, fallen, or buried and in various stages of decomposition; dung; humus; fungi, either in rotting vegetation or cultivated within the nest (as by Old World fungus–growing termites); and special or incidental items such as algae, lichens, organically rich nest materials, and, occasionally, other termites of the same colony. Most of the data reviewed by Wood are not quantitative, since they are from narrative accounts of field and laboratory observations or from analyses of food stores in nests, gut contents, or fecal material. However, a number of authors have been able to add some data by evaluating the role of subterranean termites in the detritus cycle of the Sonoran Desert. These studies on the Santa Rita Experimental Range have involved determining the rate of dead wood production, termite feeding preferences, and rates of wood consumption.

*LIVING VEGETATION.* Relatively few termites attack living vegetation (Harris 1962) and of these, only two species are found in the Sonoran Desert. *Paraneotermes simplicicornis* attacks a variety of live, cultivated young trees and shrubs, severing them at or just below ground level and above the root zone. The break can be so nearly square that the tree appears to have been sawed off. Examples range from cotton plants (*Gossypium barbadense* L.) about 1.3 cm in diameter to a young apple tree (*Malus* spp.) with the considerable trunk diameter of 11.5 cm. Plants are probably attacked in this manner in uncultivated areas although the results are not as obvious as in an urban or agricultural setting. This termite species also excavates pipes within the trunks of living trees such as *Acacia Greggii*

Gray. Light (1937) found *P. simplicicornis* in living or partly living wood
in one species of *Dalea* and one of *Atriplex*.

Workers of *T. tenuirostris* have been observed cutting irregular circles,
semicircles, and other shapes from the edges of hairy leaves of a small
honeysuckle (Caprifoliaceae) (Nutting 1970a). While this is apparently the
only record of such activity, stores of dry plant fragments found in nests of
this species (Weesner 1953; Nutting 1970a) indicate that it commonly har-
vests both living and dead plant material.

   *DEAD VEGETATION*.    Five species of drywood termites (*Pterotermes
occidentis, I. banksi, I. minor, I. seeversi*, and *Marginitermes hubbardi*)
and one dampwood termite (*Z. laticeps*) found in the Sonoran Desert forage and nest exclusively within dead wood. All subterranean species discussed in this chapter also utilize dead wood to a very large extent.

   Many of these subterranean species are polyphagous. *Paraneotermes
simplicicornis* attacks the stumps, roots, and large buried pieces of most
of the trees, shrubs, and larger cacti, but favors the riparian species such
as cottonwood, sycamore, and desert-willow (*Chilopsis linearis* [Cav.]). In
some areas this termite species is relatively common in the dying or recently
dead roots and lower trunk of mesquite, acacia (*Acacia* spp.), and cactus
skeletons, particularly those of the larger chollas and saguaro (*Carnegiea
gigantea* [Engelm.] Britt. & Rose). *Heterotermes aureus, R. tibialis*, and
*G. perplexus* are general feeders, consuming fallen and standing dead wood
and even climbing live trunks for 2 or 3 m to eat dead tissue. Of the Sonoran
Desert termites, the *Amitermes* spp. appear to be the least generalized
feeders. The meager information available suggests that, as a group, they
concentrate their attention on woody legumes, particularly roots, stumps,
and surface wood that is partly or even completely buried. However, these
species are occasionally found in the lower trunk and roots of dead cholla.
*Gnathamitermes perplexus* also very commonly feeds on standing dead
plants, particularly the stems and leaves of grasses and herbs.

   *Gnathamitermes perplexus* and *T. tenuirostris* are important litter feeders, particularly on the weathered remains of grasses and herbs. The former also feeds on the chaff dumps around nest entrances of harvester ants
in the genera *Pogonomyrmex* and *Veromessor*. *Gnathamitermes perplexus*
is occasionally found in the subsurface seed stores of these two ants, presumably seeking chaff. It is also partial to fallen cholla joints.

   Although Sonoran Desert termites tend to be generalists, they have distinct feeding preferences among the available plants. Of 13 wood species
on the Santa Rita Experimental Range, *P. simplicicornis* prefers catclaw
acacia, mesquite, and cholla stumps, while 3 *Amitermes* spp. prefer catclaw
acacia and blue palo-verde. *Heterotermes aureus* and *G. perplexus* are general feeders on all the woods, but the former prefers desert hackberry (*Celtis*

*pallida* Torr.) and cholla wood, the latter fallen cholla joints. Each termite species maintains a fairly exclusive niche through a characteristic mode of attack on a preferential selection of host woods (Haverty and Nutting 1975a).

*DUNG AND OTHER MATERIALS.*   Many termites feed on dung (Ferrar and Watson 1970). *Gnathamitermes perplexus* is often found in cattle dung as well as in that of horses, deer, rabbits, and other herbivores. *Amitermes wheeleri, A. emersoni, R. tibialis,* and *H. aureus* also feed on cattle dung to some extent. Paper products, particularly weathered cardboard cartons on roadsides and in sandy areas, are especially attractive to *G. perplexus, Amitermes* spp., and *H. aureus.*

## Production and Consumption Rates

On the Santa Rita Experimental Range, standing-crop biomass of superficial dead wood was determined to be 2,127 kg per ha, with 5 plant species representing 97.6% of the biomass and 6 accounting for 96.4% of the annual production of 450 kg per ha (Table 4.1) (Haverty and Nutting 1975b). Haverty and Nutting (1975c) constructed a simple but realistic model to simulate consumption of superficial dead wood by *H. aureus.* The model predicted that these foragers would remove dead wood from the site at the rate of 78.9 kg per ha per year, which represented 3.7% of the standing-

Table 4.1 Biomass of superficial dead-wood standing crop and annual production of dead wood on the Santa Rita Experimental Range in Arizona (modified from Haverty and Nutting 1975b)

| Wood Species | Standing Crop (est. kg/ha) | Annual Production (est. kg/ha) |
|---|---|---|
| *Acacia Greggii* | 632 | 32 |
| *Prosopis juliflora* | 360 | 159 |
| *Opuntia fulgida* | 353 | 83 |
| *Opuntia spinosior* | 312 | 15 |
| *Opuntia* spp. joints | 281 | 55 |
| *Cercidium floridum* | 138 | 70 |
| *Celtis pallida* | 17 | 1 |
| *Opuntia phaeacantha* | 10 | 20 |
| *Ephedra trifurca* | 8 | 5 |
| *Gutierrezia Sarothrae* | 8 | 9 |
| Other woods | 7 | 1 |
| Totals | 2,127 | 450 |

crop biomass and 17.5% of the annual production of dead wood. Rough estimates of dead wood removal (kg per ha per year) by *G. perplexus, P. simplicicornis, A. wheeleri,* and six other species combined are as follows: 240, 45, 25, and 25. Equivalent percentages of the annual dead wood production removed by these termites are 53.3%, 10.0%, 5.6%, and 5.6%, respectively, with the remaining 10.9% consumed by microorganisms (Nutting, Haverty, and La Fage 1975).

Silva, MacKay, and Whitford (1985) determined that *G. tubiformans* annually removed slightly more than 50% of the surface litter of a dominant perennial grass in the Chihuahuan Desert. A similar figure was obtained for this termite species in a shortgrass ecosystem in west Texas (Bodine and Ueckert 1975). While no comparable data are available, it seems likely that in the Sonoran Desert, *G. tubiformans* ecological equivalent, *G. perplexus,* must remove a large portion of the grassy litter.

## Termite Sampling Techniques

The feeding habits of a termite species ultimately influence the reliability of a sampling technique and should be a critical consideration in the technique's selection. The conventional methods for sampling subterranean termites include bait sampling and soil sampling. Problems associated with these sampling techniques have been reviewed by Sands (1972). Results obtained by bait sampling are affected by the manner in which the bait is presented, as well as by the nature and size of the bait. Soil sampling, which primarily involves pits and cores, is inherently limited by the clumped nature of most social insect populations.

Using a modification of the bait-sampling technique, La Fage, Nutting, and Haverty (1973) found that rolls of toilet paper served as a very attractive food source for the desert subterranean termites *G. perplexus* and *H. aureus.* Both species located and fed on toilet paper more quickly than on wooden blocks. Furthermore, rolls could be examined with a minimum of disturbance to termites so that the incidence of foraging could be monitored on a continuing basis. A large grid of toilet paper rolls subsequently was used to assess surface foraging populations of *H. aureus* (Haverty, Nutting, and La Fage1975) and *G. perplexus* (La Fage, Haverty, and Nutting 1976).

Haverty, Nutting, and La Fage (1976) also compared the toilet paper bait technique to the quadrat technique for determining the abundance of desert subterranean termites at the Santa Rita Experimental Range. They reported that numbers of *H. aureus* and *G. perplexus* were reasonably estimated by baiting, but that three additional termite species, *P. simplicicornis, A. wheeleri,* and *A. minimus,* were found when a series of 50 m$^2$

circular quadrats (circledrats) were examined for all termite-infested superficial and partially buried wood. Toilet paper apparently was less acceptable
simply because *P. simplicicornis* and *Amitermes* spp. feed primarily on
buried wood, and *T. tenuirostris* forages for grassy litter and herbs. However, these four species occasionally attack surface wood and have since
been found in low numbers in toilet paper baits (Jones, unpublished data).

## FORAGING ECOLOGY

Most termites forage for food and eat it as they find it. The Old World
fungus growers, however, recycle a great variety of vegetable matter by
incorporating their feces into fungus gardens, which permits a high efficiency in processing food material. Termites generally seek their food within
wood, within soil, or via aerial earthen shelters and runways. A few forage
in the open air. Foraging for food and prenuptial swarming are the primary times when termites deliberately expose themselves to the physical
environment and the threat of predation.

### Foraging Modes

All of the subterranean termite genera in the desert forage at least part
of the time by tunneling through the soil. *Paraneotermes simplicicornis*
and the *Amitermes* spp. are the most cryptic with regard to subterranean
habits since they prefer roots, stumps, and buried wood and are found
only rarely under objects on the soil surface. Indeed, *A. pallidus* is known
from only the alate caste, and no one has ever found a colony in the field.
*Amitermes minimus* and *A. silvestrianus* form heavy, encrusting galleries
over buried wood, and *A. coachellae* and *A. snyderi* build with heavy carton material within their workings.

*Heterotermes aureus*, *R. tibialis*, and *G. perplexus* apparently work near
the surface, since they are found most often beneath and within superficial dead wood. Of these species, *H. aureus* is known to drive exploratory
tunnels within a few centimeters of the surface and is thought to locate
aboveground food items by the well-defined temperature and moisture
shadows which these objects cast (Haverty, La Fage, and Nutting, unpublished observations). *Heterotermes aureus*, *R. tibialis*, and to a lesser extent,
*G. perplexus* and *Amitermes* spp., build characteristic covered runways
or tubes over inedible objects to reach food sources. *Gnathamitermes*
*perplexus* and *A. wheeleri* may also build broad tunnels and thin but extensive soil sheeting over exposed host material.

During the summer rainy season, under favorable temperature and moisture conditions, *T. tenuirostris* forages in the open for 2 m or more from small holes in the soil surface. The holes are surrounded by irregular piles of soil, from 2 to 3 cm high and up to 8 cm in diameter. This behavior has been observed at night and under overcast skies during the day (Nutting, Blum, and Fales 1974).

All genera of Sonoran Desert subterranean termites are attracted to objects on the soil surface, ranging from small stones only a few centimeters in diameter to large rocks that are barely movable. *Gnathamitermes perplexus, T. tenuirostris, A. snyderi, A. wheeleri,* and *Hoplotermes amplus* often build galleries and chambers interfacing with deeply set stones. The attraction probably involves a combination of favorable temperature and moisture conditions along with the presence of dead roots and other plant material.

## Abiotic Factors

Studies of seasonal variation in foraging behavior have concentrated on the harvester termites, which forage in the open, and on the mound-building species, rather than on the more cryptic, totally subterranean species. The latter, however, are at least as numerous and ecologically significant as the harvester and mound-builder termites (Sands 1972).

Seasonal foraging cycles of termites may be influenced by climatic factors, soil, and vegetation. To a lesser extent, they may be influenced by nutrient abundance, colony density, caste composition, and food consumption rates. Bouillon (1970) suggests that seasonal variation in foraging activity should be most noticeable in temperate regions where there is pronounced variation in climate. In spite of the complexity of the environment, which often leads to an interaction among factors, it is sometimes possible to determine the effects of isolated factors on termite distribution and abundance (Lee and Wood 1971a).

*TEMPERATURE AND MOISTURE.* Environmental factors, particularly temperature and moisture, regulate subterranean termite foraging on surface litter and dead wood. For example, *Heterotermes aureus* forages within a temperature range from 7.6 to 47.0°C (extremes measured under an object down to a soil depth of 15 cm) (La Fage, Nutting, and Haverty 1973). Haverty, La Fage, and Nutting (1974) report that the foraging activity of this species appears to be exogenously controlled by both temperature and moisture (Fig. 4.3). These authors found that the number of surface foragers at 100 toilet paper rolls (Y) at any instant was best indicated by the equation, $\ln Y = -0.985 - 0.0761\,T + 2.928\ln T + 0.327\ln R$, where T is the daily mean temperature (C°) at the toilet paper roll–soil interface and R is daily rainfall in mm. The number of foragers

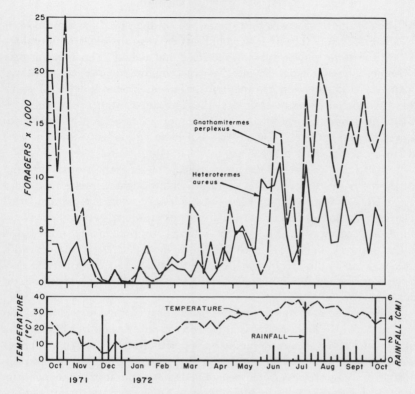

Figure 4.3. Seasonal foraging intensity of *Heterotermes aureus* and *Gnathamitermes perplexus* and accompanying temperature and rainfall for bait sampling grid, Santa Rita Experimental Range, Pima County, Arizona. The number of foragers represents the sum of 1,200 observations during 24-hour observation periods. Temperature is a daily mean at the toilet paper bait-soil interface; rainfall is a weekly total (modified from Haverty, La Fage, and Nutting 1974 and La Fage, Haverty, and Nutting 1976).

generally increased with increasing temperature, except for temperatures above 33°C, where number of foragers dramatically decreased, regardless of precipitation. From 20° to 33°C, rainfall greatly increased foraging intensity.

Foraging intensity of *G. perplexus* appears to be more strongly influenced by temperature than soil moisture (Fig. 4.3) (La Fage, Haverty, and Nutting 1976). They found that foraging intensity (number of termites at

100 toilet paper rolls) was best expressed by the equation $Y = 2.39 + 0.31\,T - 0.11\,R - 0.01\,T^2 + 0.54\ln R$, when T is daily mean temperature (C°) at the toilet paper roll–soil interface and R is daily rainfall in mm. Foraging intensity generally increased as temperature increased and was positively modified by increasing rainfall. However, short periods of heavy rain suppressed activity regardless of temperature. *Gnathamitermes perplexus* primarily foraged when soil temperatures at depths from 0 to 15 cm ranged between 9° and 49°C, but foraging intensity was curtailed at low temperatures regardless of rainfall amounts.

Both *H. aureus* and *G. perplexus* are capable of aboveground foraging for short periods at ambient temperatures a few degrees above 50°C, with *G. perplexus* having a slightly higher heat tolerance. Foragers travel upward from deep, relatively cool galleries to cavities in superficial dead wood and dung or to shelters over vegetation where they presumably exchange a load of soil for a bit of plant material. Both species pack their workings with soil, as do many other termites (Lee and Wood 1971a), and this habit may reduce or help maintain a stable temperature within these cavities (Collins et al. 1973).

Sonoran Desert termites probably are able to forage on subterranean host material throughout the year since frost rarely penetrates below the soil surface (Cable 1969). Foraging on superficial litter is occasionally limited by brief periods (hours, rarely a few days) of freezing in the more northerly areas. However, it appears that high temperatures and low moisture must regularly limit foraging for even longer periods during the dry seasons. For example, in the Arizona Upland, *Amitermes* spp. are rarely found under surface litter except during March, April, August, September, and October, when the underlying soil is moist. Since *T. tenuirostris* forages in the open at night or on cloudy days, it appears that light intensity must also influence its foraging activity within a broad temperature and moisture range.

*SOIL.*  Little is known of the effect of soil properties on Sonoran Desert termite foraging ecology. However, soil characteristics play an important role in determining the distribution and abundance of termites. The proportion of sand, silt, and clay and its distribution throughout the soil profile are particularly important for mound-building termites (Lee and Wood 1971a). Mounds are generally absent from pure sands that lack the colloidal material that termites need to cement particles together. Disturbance by seasonal cracking of soils may also prevent termites from building stable structures such as mounds and galleries (Lee and Wood 1971a). The distribution of many termites is affected by soil texture and soil depth.

Termites are important movers of soil, transporting it to the surface as they build covered runways or mounds or as they pack their workings with soil. Mounds of some termites in the savannas of Australia and Africa contain up to $2.4 \times 10^6$ kg of soil per ha (Lee and Wood 1971a). *Heterotermes aureus* and *G. perplexus* are considered to be among the primary movers of soil on the Santa Rita Experimental Range, where they are capable of moving soil at a combined rate of about 744 kg per ha per year (Nutting, Haverty, and La Fage 1987).

The foraging and building activity of termites may affect the physical and chemical characteristics of soils. In the Sonoran Desert, *H. aureus* and *G. perplexus* increase the clay content of surface soils, alter the pH from slightly acidic to basic, and enrich it with organic C, total N, Ca, Mg, K, and Na (Nutting, Haverty, and La Fage 1987). These nutrients may not be immediately available since they are released from *H. aureus* workings after months or years, but they usually are returned within weeks or months from *G. perplexus* workings. Differences in nutrient release are a consequence of the building behavior of each species. For mound-building species, the soil in the mound may be withheld from other uses for decades or even centuries (Lee and Wood 1971b).

## Biotic Factors

The importance of the flora as food for termites and their preferences for certain forms of plant material have already been discussed. The structure of the vegetation, particularly the way that it influences the amount and distribution of shade, should also be considered (Lee and Wood 1971a).

*VEGETATION.*   Vegetative patterns appear to influence foraging activity of *H. aureus* (Jones, Trosset, and Nutting 1987). Termite attack was greatest at bait sites having the most vegetative cover; the density of vegetation at attacked rolls was significantly greater ($P = 0.0204$) than at unattacked rolls. Termites may detect subsurface thermal variation between vegetated and unvegetated sites and preferentially occupy sites that contain the greatest amounts of vegetation. However, once a suitable site has been located, *H. aureus* continues to forage there, regardless of vegetative cover, until the resource has been depleted or aboveground conditions become unfavorable.

In earlier studies, Haverty and Nutting (1975b) determined that the distributions of superficial dead wood and foraging termites were aggregated. While the abundance of oligophagous species was correlated with the quantity of a highly preferred wood, there was no correlation between the abundance of polyphagous species and the quantity of any particular host wood species.

*PREDATION AND DEFENSE.*   The threat of predation and defensive strategies appear to be interdependent among the Isoptera. During and immediately after swarming, imagoes (both alates and de-alates) are eaten by various arthropods and vertebrates, including humans (Nutting 1969b). Otherwise, ants are the main predators of foraging termites. At least 33 species of ants live on the Santa Rita study site (Gaspar and Werner 1976), many of which are potential predators of termites. While the galleries of ants and termites are often found close together (as under stones, in dead wood, in toilet paper rolls, and so on), it is not clear whether any of these ants attack worker termites within the termite gallery systems. Most ants will attack exposed termites of any caste. However, F. G. Werner (personal communication) observed workers of the ant *Neivamyrmex nigrescens* (Cresson) carrying a soldier and several workers of *G. perplexus*. Lizards and birds are suspected of breaking open the earthen shelters to feed on foragers of this termite species (Asplund 1964). It is well known that blind snakes, that is, *Leptotyphlops humilis* (B. & G.) in the Sonoran Desert, feed on ants and termites (Stebbins 1966). Cactus wrens (*Campylorhynchus brunneicapillus* [Lafresnaye]) under observation near Tucson were seen feeding almost exclusively on *G. perplexus* foragers. These birds turned over plant debris and cow dung to find the termites (J. Weeks, personal communication).

*Mechanical defense.*   This type of antipredator behavior ranges from physically attacking the predator to regurgitation, defecation, abdominal dehiscence, walling off intruders, and the formation of elaborate constructions (Prestwich 1984). Contrary to popular belief, the worker caste is far from defenseless and plays a strong role in colony and foraging party defense. Workers are numerically dominant and minimally equipped with strong biting mandibles. Thorne (1982) has demonstrated that the primary function of workers is maintaining separate foraging and nesting sites in areas where termite populations are high.

Characteristic proportions of soldiers are maintained by each species for defense against intruders (Haverty 1977). Soldier mandibles have evolved in various ways for dealing with small predators: crushing, in *Paraneotermes*; slashing, in *Heterotermes* and *Reticulitermes*; and piercing, in *Amitermes* (Deligne, Quennedey, and Blum 1981). Species that depend on soldiers with such weapons maintain a relatively low percentage of soldiers but invest more energy in constructing strong nests, mounds, and foraging galleries (Prestwich 1984). This is the case with most of the subterranean species in the Sonoran Desert that forage through the soil, within wood, or under other cover: *Paraneotermes simplicicornis* maintains a mean of 11.8% soldiers; *H. aureus*, 1.5%; *R. tibialis*, 1.9%; several *Amitermes* spp., approximately 1.2%; *G. perplexus*, 1.3%; and *T. tenuirostris*, approximately 25% (Haverty 1977). The last species and other free-foraging termite species tend to maintain a high proportion of soldiers in foraging parties, presumably to enhance the defensive capabilities of the group. For a given *H. aureus* colony, a lower percentage of soldiers generally is found in large foraging groups than in small ones (Jones, unpublished data).

*Chemical defense.* Chemicals serve as important stimuli in social behavior. Among social insects, the specific odor of each colony enables colony members to recognize intruders quickly. The source of this odor may be genetic, metabolic, or derived from the environment by the odor being adsorbed onto the body. Members of a colony recognize individuals that differ in odor and typically respond antagonistically to an intruder. However, a number of authors have noted that members of separate colonies sometimes can be combined. Stuart (1969) has reviewed the literature regarding this phenomenon.

Certain genera of the Rhinotermitidae and Termitidae have soldiers adapted for chemical defense. They are equipped to apply a formidable array of irritants, contact poisons, toxicants, and glues on small arthropod predators by biting, smearing, or squirting (Prestwich 1984). Termite colonies possessing soldiers with these sophisticated chemical defenses usually have a high soldier-to-worker ratio. While they thus invest heavily in the production and maintenance of soldiers, they may invest less in heavily fortified nests and foraging galleries and may even forage in the open.

Among the Sonoran Desert termites, the chemical defense systems of *A. wheeleri* and *T. tenuirostris* have been studied. Scheffrahn et al. (1983) identified a sesquiterpene mixture from *A. wheeleri* soldier heads that acts primarily as a repellent. These authors suggest that this entirely subterranean termite species may position its relatively few soldiers in strategic peripheral locations, where they can deny ants access to the gallery system. However, they suggest that the use of solely repellent secretions would probably be inadequate to protect workers that forage in the open, as does *T. tenuirostris*.

Foraging parties of *T. tenuirostris* typically contain a few hundred individuals, 21–71% of them soldiers (Nutting, unpublished data). A column of workers several decimeters long may consist of soldiers spaced 1 or 2 cm apart and about 1 cm out from a two-way traffic of workers with as many as six abreast. Columns may branch, and termites have been observed foraging on plants at least 2 m from the nest entrance. When disturbed, outlying foragers quickly assemble toward the main column that progressively reverses its line of march, and the soldiers move in from their flanking stations to alternate with retreating groups of workers (Nutting, Blum, and Fales 1974). Traniello (1981) has shown, at least in *Nasutitermes costalis* (Holmgren), that soldiers play a key role in organizing foraging parties.

*Tenuirostritermes tenuirostris* soldiers are extremely alert to disturbances and eject a clear, sticky material from the modified "squirt gun" nasute head. They fire at close range—up to 3 mm—in the direction of vibrational or perhaps olfactory stimuli. This defensive secretion immobilized myrmicine ants (*Pheidole desertorum* Wheeler) within a few seconds in staged laboratory encounters. Three monoterpene volatiles identified from pentane extracts of the soldiers were apparently toxic to the ant victims (Nutting, Blum, and Fales 1974). No encounters between foraging groups and small arthropod predators have been observed in the field (Nutting, unpublished observations).

## TERRITORIALITY

The area occupied by a subterranean termite colony may be divided into one or more nests, often underground, and the trophic field or foraging territory centered around the nests. Bouillon (1970) points out that this territory also has depth. Termites may need to forage long distances to reach the water table, suitable construction materials, or food. The extent of each territory varies with the species, the stage of colony development, colony size, the density of required materials, and the availability of nutrients (Bouillon 1970). Coaton (1958) showed that the amount of available grass food is related to the expansion or contraction of the trophic field of *Hodotermes mossambicus* (Hagen) in South Africa. The territory of a colony may be delimited by constructions, markings from sternal and frontal gland secretions, or excrement and saliva (Bouillon 1970).

*COLONY SIZE.* The populations of mature colonies of the Kalotermitidae range from a few hundred to a few thousand individuals, while populations may number in the tens of thousands to millions in some mound-building Rhinotermitidae and Termitidae. Few attempts have been made to determine the number of individuals in a colony of the more cryptic subterranean species. In a southern Mississippi forest ecosystem, the mean colony size of *Reticulitermes flavipes* (Kollar) was estimated at about 250,000 individuals via destructive sampling techniques (Howard et al. 1982). Esenther (1980) used a Lincoln Index, mark-recapture technique, to estimate that an extensive complex of several colonies of this species numbered into the millions in Janesville, Wisconsin. Large colonies of the Formosan subterranean termite, *Coptotermes formosanus* Shiraki, are thought to exceed 1,000,000 individuals (Shimizu 1962). Available figures on colony and foraging group size for Sonoran Desert termites are summarized in Table 4.2.

The number of *Heterotermes aureus* foragers per colony has been estimated by an exhaustive trapping technique in which rolls of dampened corrugated fiberboard were fitted into polyvinyl chloride sleeves and partially buried at a site where foragers had been identified (Jones 1987).

Table 4.2 Summary of available data on colony and foraging group size for subterranean termites of the Sonoran Desert

| Species | Colony Size | Foraging Group Size (avg.) | References |
|---|---|---|---|
| *Paraneotermes simplicicornis* | 2,062 (max.) | 297 | Nutting 1970b; Haverty and Nutting 1975b |
| *Heterotermes aureus* | ~ 22,632 | 431 | Haverty, Nutting, and La Fage 1975; Haverty and Nutting 1975b |
| | 1,726 to 75,166 (range[a]) | 1,456[b] | Jones and Nutting 1987; Jones 1987 |
| | 45,000 to 300,000 (range[c]) | — | Jones 1987 |
| *Amitermes minimus* | | 152 | Haverty and Nutting 1975b |
| | | 155[b] | Jones, unpublished |
| *Amitermes wheeleri* | | 343 | Haverty and Nutting 1975b |
| *Gnathamitermes perplexus* | | 58 | Haverty and Nutting 1975b |
| | | 270[b] | Jones, unpublished |
| *Tenuirostritermes tenuirostris* | | 445 | Nutting, Blum, and Fales 1974 |

[a]Numbers collected during first year from fiberboard traps.
[b]Collected from fiberboard baits.
[c]Lincoln Index, mark-release-recapture estimates for known territories.

La Fage et al. (1983) noted that termites quickly move back into replaced traps and that a succession of traps can be used to determine population size for at least some termite species. Termites were destructively sampled and counted with a vacuum aspirator (Jones and Mauldin 1983). Within approximately one year, as many as 75,000 foragers were removed from one site, with termites continuing to forage to traps, and numbers ranged from approximately 1,700 to 41,000 termites at seven other sites (Jones and Nutting 1987). Subsequent mark-recapture studies indicated that at least 100,000 foragers remained in some of these colonies (Jones 1987). Thus, the previous estimate of approximately 23,000 termites per colony (Haverty, Nutting, and La Fage 1975) probably is an underestimate.

*FORAGING TERRITORIES.* Relatively few attempts have been made to determine the extent of the foraging territory of a termite species. Most notable are those of Nel (1968) in South Africa, Darlington (1982) in East Africa, Gay and Greaves (1940) in Australia, and King and Spink (1969) and Haverty, Nutting, and La Fage (1975) in North America.

In the Sonoran Desert, Haverty, Nutting and La Fage (1975) positioned a large grid of toilet paper baits on the soil surface to estimate the average foraging territory of *H. aureus*. The baits were placed in an overdispersed fashion without regard to microsites known to have termites. They followed territory expansion by monitoring these baits and recording mean weekly counts of termites and the lateral spread of termites to new rolls. Distinct groupings of infested rolls were considered to constitute separate colonies. Based on these criteria, 26 complete and 12 partial territories were delineated for the 40 × 40 m study site with an estimated 190.4 colonies per ha and an average foraging territory of 12.5 m². The authors qualified these estimates as perhaps being somewhat arbitrary, but suggested that their groupings might also represent subcolonies or foraging areas of much larger colonies and that additional techniques to refine estimates of territory size and number of termites per colony were needed.

Thus further research was initiated to examine the foraging ecology of Sonoran Desert termites, primarily *H. aureus*, using similar but somewhat more sophisticated techniques (Jones 1987). In 1984, field studies were begun at the Santa Rita Experimental Range. Many small plots (6 × 6 m) of 25 toilet paper rolls each, rather than one large plot, were monitored for 13 months. These baits were set out at 30 microsites known to have termites, but plots were separated from each other by at least 12 m. Of 750 rolls, *H. aureus* attacked 36.4% compared to 22.8% of the 1,681 available rolls that Haverty, Nutting, and La Fage (1975) monitored for 12 months. These numbers probably were influenced by the extra month as well as the arrangement of plots. Since rolls were deliberately situated in the vicinity of wood occupied by *H. aureus* and then substituted for the wood as the termites' food source, termite infestation of rolls would have been maximized.

Subsequent to these observations, a dye, Sudan Red 7B, was used to mark *H. aureus* foragers in order to identify the territorial extent of each colony (Jones 1987). Su, La Fage, and Esenther (1983) found that this dye was useful for studying the foraging behavior of subterranean termites because it remained in the termite tissues for several weeks and could be measured quantitatively. Such a marking material also has the advantage of being less biologically hazardous than radioactive tracers, which have been used to trace the nesting systems of subterranean species including *C. formosanus* (Li et al. 1976) and *Mastotermes darwiniensis* Froggatt (Spragg and Fox 1974; Spragg and Paton 1980).

The results of these studies indicated that *H. aureus* maintains fairly large, distinct foraging territories that are probably closely spaced in areas of abundant food (dead wood) such as the desert grasslands of southern Arizona (Jones 1987). Territories in excess of 300 m² were found for several colonies. The largest territory exceeded 3,300 m², with foragers from the same colony occurring in 5 plots. In comparison, the largest territory for 1 colony was estimated at 115 m² by Haverty, Nutting, and La Fage (1975). These data also show that *H. aureus* foragers from the same colony occupy rolls that are both spatially and temporally separated from other aggregations, often with more than one initial focus of activity. Thus, the criteria of Haverty, Nutting, and La Fage (1975) for determining colony boundaries contained several uncertainties that may have led to an overestimation of the number of *H. aureus* colonies and an underestimation of territory extent.

While we do not know whether individual *H. aureus* colonies interact in peripheral foraging zones, small groups of termites from ostensibly separate colonies react aggressively against each other under experimental conditions, whereas those from different parts of an apparently large colony do not (Jones 1987). However, lack of aggression is not always a reliable indicator of territorial boundaries . For example, there were several situations where two distinct territories were identified on the basis of recapture of dyed termites, yet individuals from these colonies were not aggressive toward each other. Since these territories were in close proximity, perhaps this is an indication that one colony had budded off from another. Neotenic reproductives, which were found for the first time in field colonies of *H. aureus* (Jones 1987), probably head such groups.

*COMPETITION.* Most termite populations appear to be affected by competition, but the role of competition in population regulation and species abundance needs additional study. According to Wood and Lee (1971), overdispersion of termite mounds suggests that competition among mound-building species is a common occurrence. They suggest that competition between colonies of *Nasutitermes exitiosus* (Hill) influences the spatial distribution of mounds. Darlington (1982) suggests that the overdispersed distribution of mature nests of *Macrotermes michaelseni* (Sjöstedt) is related to intraspecific aggression. This species apparently defends its foraging area, and storage pits filled with dead termites have been found at the junction of two colonies' foraging areas. Levings and Adams (1984) note that aggressive interactions occur when the foraging territories of two different colonies of *Nasutitermes* spp. meet. The foraging territories are defended from other colonies both intra- and interspecifically. Discrete boundaries between *Hodotermes mossambicus* (Hagen) colonies are maintained by intraspecific aggression (Nel 1968).

Interspecific and intraspecific competition thus appear to influence termite foraging patterns, but these factors previously have not been studied for Sonoran Desert termites. In our studies, we seldom found *G. perplexus* and *Heterotermes aureus* occupying the same toilet paper roll. Subsequent

analyses suggested that these two species did not forage in rolls independently of each other (Jones and Trosset, unpublished data). Not only did
*G. perplexus* depart from rolls occupied by *H. aureus*, but the effect of
this interaction was found to be of notable duration, with *G. perplexus*
taking significantly longer to return to sites occupied by *H. aureus* than to
sites that it had occupied alone. The physical nature of the interaction
between these species is unknown. However, when a roll is disturbed and
workers from the two species contact each other, fighting ensues. These
data suggest that interference competition between *H. aureus* and *G.
perplexus* occurs for a mutually satisfying food resource.

## CONCLUSIONS

We are only beginning to appreciate the many roles of termites in natural ecosystems as herbivores, detritivores, and decomposers; in recycling
dead—occasionally living—plant materials; as turners and enrichers of the
soil; and as producers of seasonal swarms of winged reproductives that form
a food source of high nutritional value for a variety of predators, both inver-
tebrate and vertebrate. The ubiquity of subterranean termites in the Sonoran
Desert has long been recognized, but only within the last decade or so
have studies of their foraging ecology been attempted. We are slowly beginning to understand the complex nature of these species with respect to
utilization of food resources, response to abiotic and biotic factors, and
partitioning of the total habitat. For example, among the Sonoran desert
termites, each species appears to maintain a fairly exclusive niche through
a characteristic mode of attack on a preferential selection of host woods.
The foraging activity of several species is critically influenced by temperature and moisture, and perhaps by a number of yet undetermined factors.
Vegetative cover appears to influence whether or not foragers investigate
a particular site. Techniques to estimate the extent of a colony's territory
are being refined, and estimates of territory size and number of termites
per colony are being revised. Such topics continue to challenge researchers
interested in understanding the role of termites in desert ecosystems.

## REFERENCES

Asplund, K. K. 1964. Seasonal variation in the diet of *Urosaurus ornatus* in a riparian com-
    munity. *Herpetologica* 20:91–94.
Axelrod, D. I. 1979. Age and origin of Sonoran Desert vegetation. Calif. Acad. Sci., Occa-
    sional Papers 132, 74 pp.

Bodine, M. C., Ueckert, D. N. 1975. Effect of desert termites on herbage and litter in a shortgrass ecosystem in west Texas. *J. Range Manag.* 28:353–58.

Bouillon, A. 1970. Termites of the Ethiopian region. In *Biology of Termites*, Vol. 2, eds. K. Krishna and F. M. Weesner, 153–280. New York: Academic. 643 pp.

Cable, D. R. 1969. Soil temperature variations on a semidesert habitat in southern Arizona. Research Note RM128. Ft. Collins: U.S. Dept. Agri. For. Serv., Rocky Mt. Stn., 4 pp.

Chamberlin, E. G., Havens, Y. H. 1970. Soil survey: a special report. IBP, Desert Biome, Santa Rita Validation Site. University of Arizona, Tucson. U.S. Dept. Agri., Soil Conserv. Serv. and Agri. Exp. Stn., 5 pp.

Coaton, W. G. H. 1958. The hodotermitid harvester termites of South Africa. Dept. Agri. Sci. Bull., Union of S. Africa, Sci. Bull. No. 375, Entomol. Ser. No. 43. 112 pp.

Collins, M. S. 1969. Water relations in termites. In *Biology of Termites*, Vol. 1, eds. K. Krishna and F. M. Weesner, 433–58. New York: Academic. 598 pp.

Collins, M. S., Haverty, M. I., La Fage, J. P., Nutting, W. L. 1973. High-temperature tolerance in two species of subterranean termites from the Sonoran Desert in Arizona. *Environ. Entomol.* 2:1122–23.

Darlington, J. P. E. C. 1982. The underground passages and storage pits used in foraging by a nest of the termite *Macrotermes michaelseni* in Kajiado, Kenya. *J. Zool.* (London) 198:237–47.

Deligne, J. A., Quennedey, A., Blum, M. S. 1981. The enemies and defense mechanisms of termites. In *Social Insects*. Vol. 2, ed. H. R. Hermann, 1–76. New York: Academic. 491 pp.

Emerson, A. E. 1955. Geographical origins and dispersions of termite genera. *Fieldiana: Zool.* 37:465–521.

Esenther, G. R. 1980. Estimating the size of subterranean termite colonies by a release-recapture technique. Proc. 11th Ann. Meet. Int. Res. Grp., Working Group I: Biol. Problems. Doc. No. IRG/WP/1112. Raleigh, NC, 4 pp.

Ferrar, P., Watson, J. A. L. 1970. Termites (Isoptera) associated with dung in Australia. *J. Aust. Entomol. Soc.* 9:100–102.

Gaspar, C., Werner, F. G. 1976. The ants of Arizona: an ecological study of ants in the Sonoran Desert. *US/IBP Desert Biome Research Memorandum 73-50*. In Reports of 1975 Progress 3:33–46.

Gay, F. J., Greaves, T. 1940. The population of a mound colony of *Coptotermes lacteus* (Frogg.). *J. Council for Scientific and Industrial Research* 13:145–63.

Harris, W. V. 1962. Classification of the phytophagous Isoptera. Symposia Genetica et Biologica Italica. Atti IV Congr. U.I.E.I.S.—Pavia, 9–14 Settembre, 1961, 11:193–201.

Haverty, M. I. 1977. The proportion of soldiers in termite colonies: a list and a bibliography. *Sociobiology* 2:199–216.

Haverty, M. I., LaFage, J. P., Nutting, W. L. 1974. Seasonal activity and environmental control of foraging of the subterranean termite, *Heterotermes aureus* (Snyder), in a desert grassland. *Life Sci.* 15:1091–1101.

Haverty, M. I., Nutting, W. L. 1975a. Natural wood preferences of desert termites. *Ann. Entomol. Soc. Amer.* 68:533–36.

————. 1975b. Density, dispersion, and composition of desert termite foraging populations and their relationship to superficial dead wood. *Environ. Entomol.* 4:480–86.

————. 1975c. A simulation of wood consumption by the subterranean termite, *Heterotermes aureus* (Snyder), in an Arizona desert grassland. *Insectes Soc.* 22:93–102.

————. 1976. Environmental factors affecting the geographical distribution of two ecologically equivalent termite species in Arizona. *Amer. Mid. Nat.* 95:20–27.

Haverty, M. I., Nutting, W. L., LaFage, J. P. 1975. Density of colonies and spatial distribution of foraging territories of the desert subterranean termite, *Heterotermes aureus* (Snyder). *Environ. Entomol.* 4:105–9.

——. 1976. A comparison of two techniques for determining abundance of subterranean termites in an Arizona desert grassland. *Insectes Soc.* 23:175–78.

Howard, R. W., Jones, S. C., Mauldin, J. K., Beal, R. H. 1982. Abundance, distribution, and colony size estimates for *Reticulitermes* spp. (Isoptera: Rhinotermitidae) in southern Mississippi. *Environ. Entomol.* 11:1290–93.

Jones, S. C. 1987. Foraging party and territory size of the desert subterranean termite *Heterotermes aureus* (Snyder) in a Sonoran Desert grassland. Ph.D. dissertation. University of Arizona, Tucson.

Jones, S. C., Mauldin, J. K. 1983. A vacuum-aspirator for counting termites. Res. Note SO-300. New Orleans: U.S. Dept. Agri. For. Serv., South. For. Exp. Stn., 2 pp.

Jones, S. C., Nutting, W. L. 1987. Size of colony and foraging territory of the desert subterranean termite, *Heterotermes aureus* (Snyder): a preliminary report. In *Chemistry and Biology of Social Insects*, eds. J. Ender and H. Rembold, 519–20. München, Germany: Verlag J. Peperny.

Jones, S. C., Trosset, M. W., Nutting, W. L. 1987. Biotic and abiotic influences on foraging of *Heterotermes aureus* (Snyder) (Isoptera: Rhinotermitidae). *Environ. Entomol.* 16:791–95.

King, E. G., Jr., Spink, W. T. 1969. Foraging galleries of the Formosan subterranean termite, *Coptotermes formosanus*, in Louisiana. *Ann. Entomol. Soc. Amer.* 62:536–42.

La Fage, J. P., Haverty, M. I., Nutting, W. L. 1976. Environmental factors correlated with the foraging behavior of a desert subterranean termite, *Gnathamitermes perplexus* (Banks) (Isoptera: Termitidae). *Sociobiology* 2:155–69.

La Fage, J. P., Nutting, W. L., Haverty, M. I. 1973. Desert subterranean termites: A method for studying foraging behavior. *Environ. Entomol.* 2:954–56.

La Fage, J. P., Su, N-Y., Jones, M. J., Esenther, G. R. 1983. A rapid method for collecting large numbers of subterranean termites from wood. *Sociobiology* 7:305–9.

Lee, K. E., Wood, T. G. 1971a. *Termites and Soils*. New York: Academic. 251 pp.

——. 1971b. Physical and chemical effects on soils of some Australian termites, and their pedological significance. *Pedbiologia* 11:376–409.

Levings, S. C., Adams, E. S. 1984. Intra- and interspecific territoriality in *Nasutitermes* (Isoptera: Termitidae) in a Panamanian mangrove forest. *J. Anim. Ecol.* 53:705–14.

Li, T., He, K-H., Gao, D-X., Chao, Y. 1976. A preliminary study of the foraging behaviour of the termite, *Coptotermes formosanus* (Shiraki) by labelling with iodine[131]. *Acta Entomol. Sin.* 19:32–38.

Light, S. F. 1930a. The California species of the genus *Amitermes* Silvestri (Isoptera). *Univ. Calif. Publ. Entomol.* (Berkeley) 5:173–214.

——. 1930b. The Mexican species of *Amitermes* Silvestri (Isoptera). *Univ. Calif. Publ. Entomol.* (Berkeley) 5:215–32.

——. 1931. The termites of Nevada. *Pan-Pac. Entomol.* 8:5–9.

——. 1932. Contributions toward a revision of the American species of *Amitermes* Silvestri. *Univ. Calif. Publ. Entomol.* (Berkeley) 5:355–414.

——. 1937. Contributions to the biology and taxonomy of *Kalotermes* (*Paraneotermes*) *simplicicornis* Banks (Isoptera). *Univ. Calif. Publ. Entomol.* (Berkeley) 6:423–64.

McGinnies, W. G., Goldman, B. J., Paylore, P., eds. 1968. *Deserts of the World: an appraisal of research into their physical and biological environments.* Tucson: University of Arizona Press. 788 pp.

Nel, J. J. C. 1968. Aggressive behaviour of the harvester termites *Hodotermes mossambicus* (Hagen) and *Trinervitermes trinervoides* (Sjöstedt). *Insectes Soc.* 15:145–56.

Nutting, W. L. 1969a. Distribution and flights of rare North American desert termites of the genus *Amitermes* (Isoptera: Termitidae). *Pan-Pac. Entomol.* 45:320–25.

——. 1969b. Flight and colony foundation. In *Biology of Termites*, Vol. 1, eds. K. Krishna and F. M. Weesner, 233–82. New York: Academic. 598 pp.

——. 1970a. Free diurnal foraging by the North American nasutiform termite, *Tenuirostritermes tenuirostris* (Isoptera: Termitidae). *Pan-Pac. Entomol.* 46:39–42.

——. 1970b. Composition and size of some termite colonies in Arizona and Mexico. *Ann. Entomol. Soc. Amer.* 63:1105–10.

Nutting, W. L., Blum, M. S., Fales, H. M. 1974. Behavior of the North American termite *Tenuirostritermes tenuirostris*, with special reference to the soldier frontal gland secretion, its chemical composition, and use in defense. *Psyche* 81:167–77.

Nutting, W. L., Haverty, M. I., La Fage, J. P. 1975. Demography of termite colonies as related to various environmental factors: Population dynamics and role in the detritus cycle. *US/IBP Desert Biome Research Memorandum 75-31.* In Reports of 1974 Progress 3:53–78.

——. 1987. Physical and chemical alteration of soil by two subterranean termite species in Sonoran Desert grassland. *J. Arid Environ.* 12:233–39.

Pickens, A. L., Light, S. F. 1934. The desert subterranean termite, *Heterotermes aureus*. In *Termites and Termite Control.* 2d Ed., ed. C. A. Kofoid, 196–98. Berkeley: University of California Press. 795 pp.

Prestwich, G. D. 1984. Defense mechanisms of termites. *Ann. Rev. Entomol.* 29:201–32.

Sands, W. A. 1972. Problems in attempting to sample tropical subterranean termite populations. *Ekol. Polksa* 20:23–31.

Scheffrahn, R. H., Gaston, L. K., Sims, J. J., Rust, M. K. 1983. Identification of the defensive secretion from soldiers of the North American termite, *Amitermes wheeleri* (Desneux) (Isoptera: Termitidae). *J. Chem. Ecol.* 9:1293–1305.

Sellers, W. D., ed. 1960. *Arizona Climate.* Tucson: University of Arizona Press, p 38.

Shimizu, K. 1962. Analytical studies on the vitality of colonies of the Formosan termite, *Coptotermes formosanus* Shiraki, I. Analysis of the strength of vitality. Miyazaki Univ., Faculty Agri., B, 8:106–10.

Shreve, F. 1964. Vegetation of the Sonoran Desert. In *Vegetation and Flora of the Sonoran Desert.* Vol. 1, eds. F. Shreve and I. L. Wiggins, 1–186. Stanford: Stanford University Press. 840 pp.

Silva, S. I., MacKay, W. P., Whitford, W. G. 1985. The relative contributions of termites and microarthropods to fluff grass litter disappearance in the Chihuahuan Desert. *Oecologia* 67:31–34.

Snyder, T. E. 1949. Catalog of the termites (Isoptera) of the world. *Smithsonian Misc. Collect.* 112:312–13.

Spragg, W. T., Fox, R. E. 1974. The use of a radiotracer to study the nesting system of *Mastotermes darwiniensis* Froggatt. *Insectes Soc.* 21:309–16.

Spragg, W. T., Paton, R. 1980. Tracing, trophallaxis and population measurement of colonies of subterranean termites (Isoptera) using a radioactive tracer. *Ann. Entomol. Soc. Amer.* 73:708–14.

Stebbins, R. C. 1966. *A Field Guide to the Western Reptiles and Amphibians.* Boston: Houghton Mifflin Co. 279 pp.

Stuart, A. M. 1969. Social behavior and communication. In *Biology of Termites*, Vol. 1, eds. K. Krishna and F. M. Weesner, 193–232. New York: Academic. 598 pp.

Su, N-Y., LaFage, J. P., Esenther, G. R. 1983. Effects of a dye, Sudan Red 7B, on the Formosan subterranean termite, *Coptotermes formosanus* Shiraki (Isoptera: Rhinotermitidae). *Mater. Org.* 18:127–33.

Thorne, B. L. 1982. Termite-termite interactions: workers as an agonistic caste. *Psyche* 89:133–50.

Traniello, J. F. A. 1981. Enemy deterrence in the recruitment strategy of a termite: soldier-organized foraging in *Nasutitermes costalis*. *Proc. Natl. Acad. Sci.* (USA) 78:1976–79.

Turner, R. M., Brown, D. E. 1982. Sonoran desertscrub. In *Biotic Communities of the American Southwest-United States and Mexico*. Ed. D. E. Brown, *Desert Plants*, 4(1–4): 181–221. Tucson: University of Arizona. 342 pp.

Weesner, F. M. 1953. The biology of *Tenuirostritermes tenuirostris* (Desneux) with emphasis on caste development. *Univ. Calif. Publ. Zool.* (Berkeley) 57:251–302.

Wood, T. G. 1978. Food and feeding habits of termites. In *Production Ecology of Ants and Termites*. Ed. M. V. Brian, 55–80. Cambridge, England: Cambridge University Press. 409 pp.

Wood, T. G., Lee, K. E. 1971. Abundance of mounds and competition among colonies of some Australian termite species. *Pedobiologia* 11:341–66.

# 5

# SPINES AND VENOMS IN FLORA AND FAUNA IN THE ARIZONA UPLAND SONORAN DESERT AND HOW THEY ACT AS DEFENSES AGAINST VERTEBRATES

## Justin O. Schmidt

Southwestern Biological Institute
Tucson, Arizona

## SPINY AND VENOMOUS FLORA AND FAUNA IN THE ARIZONA UPLAND SONORAN DESERT (AUSD)

The area considered in this presentation is the Arizona Upland subdivision of the Sonoran Desert (Figure 5.1) as delineated by Turner and Brown (1982). The term *spine* is used loosely and is intended to include any plant part (thorn, spine, glochidium, leaf point, and so forth) capable of penetrating the flesh of a human or other animal and which appears designed for such penetration. This excludes broken plant parts, dead "snags," and branches. The term *venom* is used to describe any naturally produced material that is injected into a target organism and is capable of causing pain, toxicity, tissue damage, or some specific effect in the target organism. Toxins produced by plants or animals that are active primarily when ingested are not considered to be venoms.

### Plants of the Arizona Upland Sonoran Desert (AUSD)

The plants considered in this chapter are woody and suffrutescent (subshrub) perennials. These plants comprise most of the long-term living biomass of the environment and are generally the largest species. Annuals and herbs are excluded from this presentation.

The dominant woody and suffrutescent perennial plants in the AUSD are listed in Table 5.1. Also noted in the table is the nature of the arma-

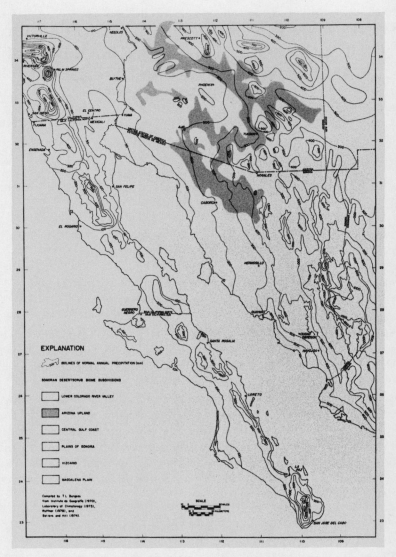

Figure 5.1.    The Arizona Upland Sonoran Desert region on
the Sonoran Desert. Map courtesy of Ray Turner.

ture of these plants. Of the 72 species listed in the table, 32, or 44%, are armed with some sort of spines, thorns, or other sharp structures. Of the more abundant species (listed in Table 5.1 as abundances C–A to very A), 56% are armed, while of the less abundant species (listed as from U to C) 33% are armed. In the largest plants, trees, and tree succulents, 90% of the species are armed whereas only 30% of the shrub and 7% of the sub-shrub species are armed. Armature occurs in 86% of the remaining species (succulents, vines, parasites), a figure primarily resulting from the dominance of cacti.

Based on the data in Table 5.1, the AUSD is an area inhabited by a great array of spiny plants. The question arises, how does the spinescence of the AUSD plants compare to that of plants from other parts of North America? For comparison, the Great Smoky Mountains of Tennessee and North Carolina represent an eastern North American ecosystem that is at about the same latitude as the AUSD, but this ecosystem is a deciduous forest that receives much greater rainfall than the AUSD. Perusal of the vegetative data in this area typical of eastern North America reveals that there are very few plants that are spiny or armed (Whittaker 1956). Like-wise, the vegetation of the Siskiyou Mountains of Oregon and California, a Pacific mixed evergreen forest, contains very few spiny plants (Whitta-ker 1960). The vegetation of the great North American prairies is mostly grass interspersed with nonspiny herbs and trees. The above areas con-tain more moisture than the AUSD. An area equally dry as the AUSD, but colder, is the Great Basin Desert just north of the AUSD in Nevada, Utah, Colorado, Wyoming, Idaho, western Montana, and northern New Mexico and Arizona. This desert is dominated by sagebrushes (*Artemisia*), saltbrushes (*Atriplex*), blackbrush (*Coleogyne*), winterfat (*Ceratoides*), greasewood (*Sarcobatus*), rabbitbrush (*Chrysothamnus*), and so forth, all spineless shrubs (Turner and Brown 1982). The AUSD is thus spiny rela-tive to temperate North American areas.

## Venomous Animals of the Arizona Upland Sonoran Desert

Animals, unlike plants, have the ability to move and can frequently direct defenses toward their predators. For these and other reasons animals have tended to evolve venoms rather than spines as defenses. Venoms can be housed in mobile piercing devices that can be thrust into or aimed at a predator. There are also some animals with immobile venomous spines; for example, some caterpillars have venomous spines permanently attached to their integuments. In general, though, these types of venom apparatus are less common than ones that are mobile. In this chapter, discussions of venomous animals will be limited to those using their venoms, at least in part, for defense against vertebrate predators.

Table 5.1.  Dominant nonherbaceous perennial plants of the Arizona Upland Sonoran Desert[1,2]

| Species | Common Name | Abundance[3] | Size | Armature[4] |
|---|---|---|---|---|
| Abutilon incanum | | C | shrub | |
| Acacia constricta | whitethorn acacia | C–A | shrub | S |
| A. greggii | catclaw acacia | A | shrub | RS |
| Aloysia wrightii | aloysia | C | shrub | |
| Ambrosia ambrosioides | canyon ragweed | C–A | shrub | |
| A. deltoidea | triangle-leaf bursage | Very A | shrub | |
| Anisacanthus thurberi | desert honeysuckle | U–C | shrub | |
| Baccharis sarothroides | desert broom | C–A | shrub | |
| Bebbia juncea | chuckwalla's delight | C–A | shrub | |
| Beloperone californica | chuparosa | U | shrub | |
| Brickellia coulteri | bricklebush | C | subshrub | |
| Calliandra eriophylla | fairy duster | C | shrub | |
| Canotia holacantha | crucifixion thron | U | shrub/tree | SB |
| Carlowrightia arizonica | | C | shrub | |
| Carnegiea gigantea | saguaro | A–Very A | tree succulent | S |
| Cassia covesii | desert senna | C | subshrub | |
| Castela emoryi | crucifixon thorn | C–A | shrub/tree | SB |
| Celtis pallida | desert hackberry | C–A | shrub | S |
| Cercidium floridum | blue palo verde | A (washes) | tree | S |
| C. microphyllum | little-leaf palo verde | Very A | tree | SB |
| Chilopsis linearis | desert willow | C (washes) | tree | |
| Commicarpus scandens | | C | subshrub | |
| Condalia warnockii | condalia | C | shrub | SB |
| Coursetia microphylla | | C–A (local) | shrub | |
| Crossosoma bigelovii | crossosoma | C | shrub | |
| Dodanaea viscosa | hopbush | C–A | shrub | |
| Echinocereus fasciculatus | hedgehog cactus | C | stem succulent | S |
| Encelia farinosa | brittlebush | A | shrub | |
| Ephedra spp. | Mormon tea | C | shrub | |
| Ericameria laricifolia | terpentine bush | C–A | shrub | |
| Eriogonum wrightii | Wright buckwheat | C | shrub | |
| Ferrocactus wislizenii | barrel cactus | C | stem succulent | S |
| Fouquieria splendens | ocotillo | A | shrub | S |
| Galium stellatum | desert bedstraw | C | subshrub | |
| Gutierrezia sarothrae | snakeweed | C | subshrub | |
| Hibiscus coulteri | hibiscus | C | subshrub | |
| H. denudatus | hibiscus | C | subshrub | |
| Hymenoclea monogyra | burrobush | A | shrub | |
| Hyptis emoryi | desert lavender | C | shrub | |
| Isocoma tenuisecta | burro-weed | C–A | subshrub | |
| Janusia gracilis | janusia | C–A | vine | |
| Jatropha cardiophylla | limberbush | C–A | shrub | |
| Krameria grayi | white ratany | C | shrub | SB |
| K. parvifolia | range ratany | C | shrub | SB |
| Larrea divaricata | cresotebush | very A | shrub | |
| Lophocereus schottii | senita cactus | C–A (local) | tree succulent | S |

Table 5.1. Dominant nonherbaceous perennial plants of the Arizona Upland Sonoran Desert[1,2] (Continued)

| Species | Common Name | Abundance[3] | Size | Armature[4] |
|---|---|---|---|---|
| Lycium berlandieri | wolfberry | C–A | shrub | SB |
| L. exsertum | wolfberry | A | shrub | SB |
| Mammillaria microcarpa | fishhook pincushion | C–A | stem succulent | S |
| Menodora scabra | broom twinberry | C–A | subshrub | |
| Olneya tesota | desert ironwood | A | tree | RS |
| Opuntia acanthocarpa | buckhorn cholla | A | stem succulent | S |
| O. arbuscula | pencil cholla | C | stem succulent | S |
| O. bigelovii | teddy bear cholla | C–A | stem succulent | S |
| O. fulgida | chain fruit cholla | A | stem succulent | S |
| O. leptocaulis | Christmas cholla | C | stem succulent | S |
| O. phaeacantha | Engelmann prickly pear | A | stem succulent | S |
| O. stanlyi | devil's ground cholla | C | stem succulent | S |
| O. versicolor | staghorn cholla | A | stem succulent | S |
| Phoradendron californicum | desert mistletoe | C–A | parasite | |
| Porophyllum gracile | | C | subshrub | |
| Prosopis velutina | velvet mesquite | very A | tree | S |
| Psilostrophe cooperi | paper flower | C | subshrub | |
| Simmondsia chinensis | jojoba | C–A | shrub | |
| Solanum elaeagnifolium | white horse nettle | C | subshrub | S |
| Sphaeralcea sp. | globe mallow | C | subshrub | |
| Stenocereus thurberi | organ pipe | C–A (local) | tree succulent | S |
| Trixis californica | | C | shrub | |
| Yucca elata | soaptree yucca | U–C | rosette succulent | SL |
| Viguiera deltoidea | desert sunflower | C | subshrub | |
| Zinnia acerosa | desert zinnia | C | subshrub | |
| Ziziphus obtusifolia | grey thorn | C | shrub | SB |

[1]Data from Kearney and Peebles 1960; Whittaker and Niering 1965, 1968; Bowers 1980; Lane 1981; Goldberg and Turner 1986; Bowers and McLaughlin 1987
[2]Except permanent riparian habitats
[3]Abbreviations: A = abundant, C = common, U = uncommon
[4]Abbreviations: S = spines, SB = spinescent branch tips, RS = recurved spines, SL = spiny leaves

Table 5.2 lists the venomous vertebrates in the AUSD. The AUSD contains 42% of the venomous snake species and 20% of the subspecies found in the continental United States. The area also possesses 2 of the only 3 venomous subspecies of lizards in the world. Venoms are unknown from birds and amphibians (though some of the latter possess potent toxins [Flier et al. 1980; Erspamer et al. 1984]) and no U.S. mammals possess venoms of known defensive value.

Most information available on vertebrate-active arthropod venoms is derived from their effects on humans. Nevertheless, often even in the case

Table 5.2 Venomous reptiles in the Arizona Upland Sonoran Desert (AUSD)[1]

| Taxon | Common name |
| --- | --- |
| *Crotalus atrox* | Western diamondback rattlesnake |
| *C. cerastes cercobombus* | Sonoran sidewinder |
| *C. c. laterorepens* | Colorado desert sidewinder |
| *C. mitchelli pyrrhus* | Speckled rattlesnake |
| *C. molossus molossus* | Black-tailed rattlesnake |
| *C. s. scutulatus* | Mojave rattlesnake |
| *C. tigris* | Tiger rattlesnake |
| *C. virdis cerberus* | Arizona black rattlesnake |
| *Micruroides euryxanthus* | Arizona coral snake |
| *Heloderma s. suspectum* | Reticulated gila monster |
| *H. s. cinctum* | Banded gila monster |

| Totals: | USA | AUSD (% of USA total) | |
| --- | --- | --- | --- |
| Snake subspecies | 44 | 9 | (20) |
| Snake species | 19 | 8 | (42) |
| Lizard subspecies | 2 | 2 | (100) |

[1]Based on Stebbins 1985, Conant 1958, Glenn and Straight 1982, Lowe, Schwalbe, and Johnson 1986.

of humans, little is known. For example, the number of spider species that possess vertebrate-active venoms is unknown. Until recently the general consensus was that in the United States only the (black) widow and recluse spiders were venomous, but findings by Russell suggest perhaps many more species are toxic to vertebrates (Russell and Gertsch 1983; Russell 1986). Likewise, for insects many species are known to be venomous but others are only suspected of having venoms (Schmidt 1982).

Venoms of virtually all scorpions are vertebrate active. All species are capable of inflicting at least painful stings in humans. A listing of the scorpions capable of inflicting painful or toxic stings to vertebrates is given in Table 5.3. The taxonomy of scorpions is poorly known, in large part because they are not economically important. By best estimates, the AUSD area contains approximately 12 species of scorpions, or 16% of the U.S. total.

Almost all spiders are venomous to at least their prey. However, the number of spider species possessing vertebrate-active venoms is unknown and a detailed listing of these spiders must await toxinological studies. The only two genera in the United States that are commonly recognized as having potent mammalian-toxic venoms are the black widows (*Latrodec-*

Table 5.3 Venomous scorpions in, or likely to be in, the Arizona Upland Sonoran Desert (AUSD)

| | |
|---|---|
| *Centruroides exilicauda* | *Vaejovis confusus* |
| | *V. hirsuticauda* |
| *Hadrurus arizonensis* | *V. spinigerus* |
| | *V. vorhiesi* |
| *Superstitionia donensis* | |
| | *Paruroctonus boreus* |
| *Serradigitus joshuaensis* | *P. mesaensis* |
| *S. subtilimanus* | *P. stahnkei* |

| General totals: | USA[1] | AUSD[1,2] | (% of US Total) |
|---|---|---|---|
| *Centruroides* | 6 | 1 | (17) |
| *Diplocentrus* | 3 | 0 | (0) |
| *Hadrurus* | 3 | 1 | (33) |
| *Superstitionia* | 1 | 1 | (100) |
| *Serradigitus* | 6 | 2 | (33) |
| *Vaejovis* | 29 | 4 | (14) |
| *Paruroctonus* | 22 | 3 | (14) |
| *Anuroctonus* | 1 | 0 | (0) |
| *Uroctonus* | 3 | 0 | (0) |
| Overall total | 74 | 12 | (16) |

[1]W. David Sissom, personal communication
[2]Stanley C. Williams, personal communication

*tus*) and the recluse spiders (*Loxosceles*). Of these spiders, 1 of 4 widow and 3 of 14 recluse species inhabit the AUSD (Table 5.4).

Like spiders, essentially all centipedes are venomous to their prey. The use and effectiveness of their venoms as defenses against vertebrates are unclear: the only centipedes definitely venomous to vertebrates are the scolopendrids. These large centipedes (up to 20 cm long in the United States) produce painful and even lethal effects of their bites in humans (Minelli 1978). The taxonomy of centipedes including scolopendrids is in such poor shape that no reasonable estimate of the number of species in the United States is available, or even how many species exist in the AUSD (R. M. Shelley, personal communication). Large scolopendrids are, however, fairly common in the AUSD.

Insects are numerically the most abundant animals with vertebrate-active venoms. Of the insects, the main order with venomous members is the Hymenoptera (ants, wasps, and bees). Other insect orders, including the Hemiptera, Lepidoptera, Diptera, and Coleoptera, contain a few species that are venomous to vertebrates, but their anthropogenic importance is

114          *Justin O. Schmidt*

Table 5.4 Venomous spiders native to the Arizona Upland
Sonoran Desert (AUSD)[1] and the United States

| Taxa in ASUD | Taxa in the USA |
|---|---|
| *Latrodectus hesperus* | *L. bishopi, L. hesperus, L. mactans,* |
| | *L. variolus + ? others* |
| *Loxosceles arizonica*[2] | *L. apachea, L. arizonica, L. belli,* |
| *L. deserta* | *L. blanda, L. deserta, L. devia,* |
| *L. sabina* | *L. kaiba, L. laeta, L. martha,* |
| | *L. palma, L. reclusa, L. refescens,* |
| | *L. russelli, L. sabia (n = 14)* |

[1]Many other spider species are known to have milder effects on humans
(that is, Russell and Gertsch 1983; Russell 1986), but data on these
species are fragmentry and are not included.
[2]*Loxosceles* data from Gertsch and Ennik 1983.

generally small in comparison to the Hymenoptera so they will not be discussed further (for discussions of these groups, see Schmidt 1982 and Delgado Quiroz 1978). The numbers of venomous Hymenoptera in the AUSD
and in the United States are listed in Table 5.5. The decision of which
species to include in the table is difficult to make and, to a certain extent,
is arbitrary. Nevertheless, the table includes most species with highly active
venoms, though a few species in the Pompilidae, Bethylidae, and so on,
that sometimes are able to produce painful stings are omitted (all pompilids
can cause at least some pain, but those in the Pepsinae generally produce
the greatest pain). Table 5.5 is a listing of the venomous species by genus,
subfamily, and family. In this way, comparisons between numbers of species in the AUSD and in the United States can be made at various taxonomic levels. All social wasps, including the paper wasps (mainly *Polistes*
in the Polistinae) and the yellowjackets (*Paravespula* and *Vespula*) and aerial
hornets (including the baldfaced hornet (*Dolichovespula*) in the Vespinae),
possess painful venoms. Most are also highly toxic and lethal to mammals
(Schmidt 1983, 1986a; Schmidt and Blum 1979; Schmidt, Blum, and Overal
1980, 1986; Schmidt et al. 1986) Nine of the 51 U.S. species in the Vespidae,
or 18%, are residents of the AUSD. None of the 17 yellowjackets and their
relatives is found in the AUSD.

Ants are by far the most abundant and dominant of the venomous insects.
Seven subfamilies of ants, three of which possess stinging species that produce pain, live in the United States. The most primitive of these, the
Ponerinae, are most abundant in the tropics. Nevertheless, 6 U.S. species
can give painful stings to humans, one of which, *Odontomachus desertorum,*

Table 5.5 Venomous Hymenoptera in the Arizona Upland Sonoran Desert (AUSD) and in the United States[1,2]

| | Taxa in AUSD | Taxa in the U.S. | % of U.S. Total in AUSD |
|---|---|---|---|
| Vespidae (Social wasps) | | | |
|   Polistinae (paper wasps) | | | |
|     *Polistes* | 8 | 26 | 31 |
|     Other Polistinae[3] | 1 | 8 | 12 |
|       Total Polistinae | 9 | 34 | 26 |
|   Vespinae (yellowjackets) | 0 | 17 | 0 |
|        Total social wasps | 9 | 51 | 18 |
| Formicidae (ants) | | | |
|   Ponerinae[4] | 1 | 6 | 17 |
|   Pseudomyrmecinae (*Pseudomyrmex*) | 2 | 4 | 50 |
|   Myrmecinae | | | |
|     *Pogonomyrmex* (harvester ants) | 8 | 20 | 40 |
|     *Solenopsis* (fire ants) | 2 | 3 | 67 |
|       Total Myrmecinae | 10 | 23 | 43 |
|       Total ants | 13 | 33 | 39 |
| Apidae (bumblebees, *Bombus*) | 1 | 42 | 2 |
| Anthophoridae (digger bees)[5] | 5 | 14 | 36 |
| Mutillidae (Velvet wasps) | | | |
|   *Dasymutilla* | 35 | 139 | 25 |
|   *Timulla* | 6 | 38 | 16 |
|   *Pseudomethoca* | 8 | 43 | 19 |
|     Total velvet wasps | 49 | 220 | 22 |
| Pompilidae (Spider wasps)[6] | | | |
|   *Pepsis* & *Hemipepsis* | 12 | 22 | 55 |
|   Others[7] | 14 | 136 | 10 |
|     Total spider wasps | 26 | 158 | 16 |
| Total Hymenoptera | 103 | 519 | 20 |

[1]Species and subspecies as listed in Krombein et al. 1979; localities based upon data in Krombein et al. 1979; Mickel 1928, 1935; Creighton 1950; University of Arizona collection; and personal observations of author and associates.
[2]Only those species known to produce painful envenomations in humans are listed (see text for details).
[3]*Mischocyttarus, Brachygastra, Polybia.*
[4]*Platythyrea, Pachycondyla, Odontomachus.*
[5]Only *Xylocopa.*
[6]Only Pepsinae.
[7]*Chirodamus, Priocnessus, Entypus, Crytoocheilus, Calicurgus, Dipogon, Phanagenia, Auplopus, Priocnemella.*

lives in the AUSD. The Pseudomyrmecinae are a small subfamily of thin, wasplike ants that are best known for the species that mutualistically inhabit and defend neotropical bullhorn acacia plants against herbivores and most assailants (Janzen 1966). Of the four painfully stinging species native to the United States, two live in the AUSD. The subfamily Myrmicinae is the largest subfamily of stinging ants. In the United States only two genera, the harvester ants of the genus *Pogonomyrmex* and the fire ants in the genus *Solenopsis*, frequently sting humans. Both of these painfully stinging groups are well represented in the AUSD. Overall, 13 of the 33 (39%) painfully stinging ant species in the United States are present in the AUSD.

Bees are extremely abundant, both in numbers of species and of individuals. Most are small, essentially harmless species, but two native genera, *Bombus* (bumble bees) and *Xylocopa* (carpenter bees), live in the United States and can deliver painful stings. Many other bees can sting if grasped or pinched (for example, sweat bees in the Halictidae), but none of these species produce substantial pain. Bumble bees are poorly represented with only *Bombus sonorus* of the 42 U.S. species living in the AUSD. Carpenter bees, on the other hand, are well represented with 36% of the U.S. species inhabiting the AUSD.

The remaining three families in Table 5.5 represent the soitary wasps that are capable of delivering painful stings to humans and which are taxonomically known and frequently encountered. The Mutillidae is an immense family of perhaps 8,000 or more described worldwide species. These solitary wasps, often called velvet "ants," are characterized as having wingless, hard-bodied, often colorful and fuzzy-appearing females that run rapidly across the ground and that can deliver painful stings (Schmidt and Blum 1977). There are three main diurnal genera in the United States (plus many extremely poorly known nocturnal genera) that number approximately 220 species whose females are described. Forty-nine, or 22% of these species, inhabit the AUSD. Of interest is the fact that most of these AUSD species are extremely brightly colored and conspicuous (aposematic), unlike most of the species that live east of the Mississippi River.

Virtually all of the spider wasps in the family Pompilidae can deliver painful stings. The most profoundly painful of these wasps are the large species in the subfamily Pepsinae. For this reason, only this subfamily is included in Table 5.5. The largest spider wasps, the tarantula hawks in the genera *Pepsis* and *Hemipepsis*, are colored an iridescent "gun metal" blue to blue-black, often with contrasting brilliant orange wings. These wasps possess long stings that are extremely painful. Over half of the tarantula hawk species in the United States live in the AUSD. The remaining 136 species in the subfamily Pepsinae are smaller and less conspicuous. Of these, 10% inhabit the AUSD.

## PROTECTIVE MECHANISMS OF SPINES AND VENOMS

### How Spines Protect Against Herbivores

Spines deter large herbivores mainly by causing pain. In particular, the mouth, nose, and eyes as well as the surrounding area of vertebrate herbivores are usually soft, sensitive areas rich with pain receptors. Spines cause pain in any or a combination of five ways: puncturing, ripping or tearing, barbs, venoms, and infection. Many spines are hard and sharp, and they readily cause puncture wounds that often result in painful bleeding wounds. These straight spines typically act by piercing tissues directly (Figure 5.2). Recurved spines, such as are on catclaw acacias (*Acacia greggii*) and ironwood trees (*Olneya tesota*), impale the flesh of moving animals, and the curvature causes the spines to penetrate deeper as the animal pulls away (Figure 5.2). These spines become "hooked" in the flesh and can cause tears and rips as the animal moves onward. This kind of painful damage can be inflicted on an animal that is even casually moving through an area.

A sharp, clean puncture or tear causes less pain than one that produces a ragged wound. The increased pain of ragged wounds is one principle behind the increased algogenicity of barbed spines over smooth spines. Barbs such as those on the cacti, especially *Opuntia* spp., cause intense pain in humans. The exact causes of this pain has not been investigated, but both the increased tissue damage due to the backward pointing barbs and the persistence of the spine itself in the wound are factors. Many animals have difficulty removing barbed cactus spines (Figure 5.3), and this property maintains a much longer duration of pain in the animal than a simple puncture. In fact, barbs seem to be ideally suited to firmly attach to the tough, elastic integuments of vertebrates, especially mammals and birds, but also oral tissues of lizards. Many *Opuntia* species have thin membranous sheaths around their spines (Figure 5.4). The exact function of these is unclear, but they might aid in defense either by protecting the barbs from the weather or from becoming clogged with dust particles, or they might protect some type of venom.

The prevalence of venomous spines in AUSD plants is uncertain. Nettles, well-known venomous plants (Urticaceae), are rare in the AUSD, and most of the other spiny plant species do not belong to groups noted for venomous spines. Spine punctures by chollas (*Opuntia* spp.) and many agaves (*Agave* spp.) cause intense, long-lasting pain (author's observations and those of many associates). These punctures seem to cause much more pain than, for example, punctures from saguaro cactus spines or from common sewing needles. Whether this effect is due to venoms on these spines or simply to barbs is unknown and untested.

Figure 5.2.   *a*, Straight sharp piercing spines of *Zisiphus obtusifolia* (note the impaled honey bee [*Apis mellifera*]) that is a part of a shrike's [*Lanius* sp.] larder; *b*, recurved spines of ironwood (*Olneya tesota*).

Figure 5.3.   Cactus (*Opuntia* sp.) pad held by barbed spines
in the skin of a large herbivore. Herbivores such as this also
serve as dispersal agents for these vegetative reproductive
parts of the cactus.

A final and delayed-action defensive benefit of spines is the occasional
production of infection in a puncture wound by a spine. Barbed spines
that are retained in the flesh are particularly likely to cause wound infection. The infected part, often the oral area, becomes swollen and tender,
possibly rendering feeding difficult. Even if on an extremity, an infection
might decrease feeding by reducing the animal's movement. Vertebrate
herbivores are intelligent and capable of associating delayed effects such
as poisoning or infection (learned aversions) with the causative agents (Islam
1979; Bernstein and Sigmundi 1980). Thus, spine-induced infection is a
good feedback-based plant defense against large herbivores.

## How Venoms Protect Against Large Predators

In this section the physiological and behavioral basis of the protective
value of venoms against large predators will be analyzed. The principles
involved are essentially universal throughout the world of venoms, but

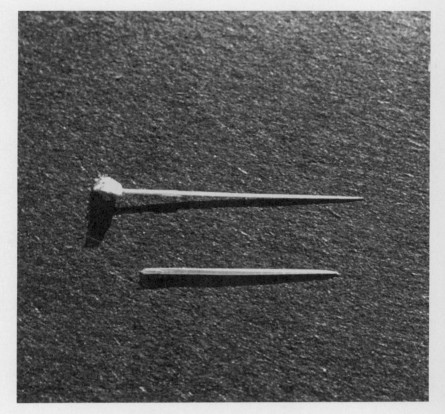

Figure 5.4. Spine from *Opuntia phaeacantha* with the spine sheath removed.

will be illustrated with venoms produced by venomous animals from the AUSD. Venoms can be of defensive value through a variety of actions including pain production, damage or death, allergy, and possession of unpleasant allomonal tastes. By far the major defensive actions are pain production and tissue damage.

The pain following envenomation is a positive and immediate signal to a predator that his potential prey animal is armed and can defend itself. Pain is essentially the sensory signal within an organism that informs it that bodily damage is occurring, has occurred, or is about to occur. As such, it is an exquisitely effective signal—for its own health, safety, and survival, an organism must note and act upon pain. Otherwise the organism is at severe risk of suffering damage and possible life-threatening results from the injurious process being signaled by the pain. A normal reponse to pain

that occurs during a predatory attack is to halt the attack and at least investigate the cause of the pain. Flight is frequently another response. All of
these predator responses are of value to a potential prey: when a stung
predator opens its mandibles or otherwise releases the prey, the prey frequently can escape before the predator recovers from the pain to possibly
continue the attack.

In addition to its immediate attack-stopping effects, pain often produces
long-term beneficial effects for the venomous prey. A predator in pain from
a sting (or other means) is likely to be moving and acting in unusual ways,
for example, flight or distraction and scratching at the sting site. These
actions can gain the attention of the predator's own predators, putting the
former at increased risk. The elimination of a predator that has just been
repelled by a venomous sting can only be beneficial to the immediate safety
and survival of the venomous prey. The main long-term benefit of pain is
that the predator, even if successful, will remember the painful encounter
and is likely to avoid further stinging encounters with organisms that look
the same. This is particularly of value to surviving nestmates of an attacked
colony (for an example where this defense fails, see Chapter 2 by P. J.
Schmidt, J. O. Schmidt, and W. C. Sherbrooke in this volume). Even
when total avoidance of the prey does not occur, if alternative food is available, a predator is likely to try to exploit that prey first before approaching
the stinging prey.

Quantitative measurement of pain is essentially impossible. This is partly
because pain is a subjective experience that differs from individual to individual and even within an individual at different times or under different
conditions. Even if the electrical output form sensory nerves could be measured, pain is a sensation in the central nervous system that is the result of
both the output from the sensory nerves and the "screening" and modula-
tion of this output by other nervous centers. Brain-produced (endorphins
and so forth) and other body hormones (adrenalin) also dramatically affect
the sensation of pain. For all these reasons, my colleagues and I (Schmidt,
Blum, and Overal 1984; Starr 1985) have developed a semiquantitative
measure of pain based on human responses to stings as ranked on a scale
of from 0 to 4. In this scale, 0 means the venom apparatus cannot penetrate the skin, a 2 is the value resulting from a typical honeybee sting (the
most common sting reference for most people), and 4 is excruciating and
debilitating pain so intense that virtually all other conscious actions are
impeded until the pain decreases. Table 5.6 is a listing of the relative pain
of stings from Hymenoptera from the AUSD. No other group of organisms is included, partly because the author has not been stung or bitten
by arachnids or snakes, and partly because these organisms can inflict potentially dangerous as well as painful envenomations.

Table 5.6 Relative painfulness of stings of Hymenoptera inhabiting the AUSD

| Family | Species | Relative Immediate Sting Pain | Duration of Pain | References[1] |
|---|---|---|---|---|
| | Solitary Hymenoptera | | | |
| Pompilidae (spider wasps) | | | | |
| | *Pepsis formosa pattoni* | 4 | 2–5 min | a |
| | other species | 2–4 | short | a |
| Mutillidae (mutillid wasps) | | | | |
| | *Dasymutilla klugii* | 3 | short (usually) | a |
| | other species | 1–3 | short | a |
| Sphecidae (sphecid wasps) | | | | |
| | largest species | 0–1 | short | b |
| Apoidea (bee superfamily) | | | | |
| | small bees in general | 0–1 | short | b |
| Anthophoridae (digger bees) | | | | |
| | *Centris pallida* | 1–2 | short | a |
| | *Didasia rinconis* | 1–2 | short | a |
| | *Habropoda pallida* | 1 | short | b |
| | *Xenoglossa angustior* | 1 | short | b |
| | *Xylocopa varipuncta* | 2 | short | b |
| | Social Hymenoptera | | | |
| Apidae (social bees) | | | | |
| | *Apis mellifera* (introduced) | 2 | 4–10 min | a |
| | *Bombus sonorus* | 2 | 2–5 min | a |
| Vespidae (social wasps) | | | | |
| | *Mischocyttarus flavitarsus* | 1–2 | 2–5 min | b |
| | *Polistes arizonensis* | 2–3 | 4–10 min | a |
| Formicidae (ants) | | | | |
| | *Odontomachus haematodus* | 2 | 4–10 min | a |
| | *Pogonomyrmex maricopa* species complex | 3 | intense 1–4 hr, less to 12 hr | a,b |
| | *P. barbatus* species complex | 3 | intense to 1 hr, less to 4 hr | a,b |
| | *Solenopsis xyloni* | 1 | 2–5 min | b |

[1]a = Schmidt 1986a; b = Schmidt, unpublished.

Any of the venoms in Table 5.6 with the ability to produce a pain level of 2 or more would be expected to have great defensive value against any size of predator. Those with pain levels lower than 2 would have stings that are likely very effective against small birds, lizards, and mammals, the predatory groups that would be expected to be the most likely attackers of these usually solitary and/or small hymenopterans.

The most painfully stinging insects in the United States are in decreasing order: the tarantula hawks (*Pepsis* and *Hemipepsis*), the harvester ants (*Pogonomyrmex*), the mutillid wasps of the genus (*Dasymutilla*, and the paper wasps (*Polistes*) and yellowjackets (Vespinae), which are about equal. Members of four of these five groups including the three most painful groups are exceedingly well represented in the AUSD. The percentages of the U.S. species in these groups that live in the AUSD are 55% of tarantula hawks, 40% of the harvester ants, 25% of the *Dasymutilla* species, and 31% of the paper wasps (Table 5.5).

The second of the two major ways a venom has defensive action is by causing damage to the envenomed potential predator. Damage can take the form of direct destruction of blood or tissues (skin, muscle, nerve, and so on), the causation of kidney malfunction, the production of necrotic lesions or infections, or death. Damage is of defensive value because it reduces the predator's ability to move and act optimally. The result is possible impairment of its ability to obtain food and its reduced ability to detect, avoid, and defend against its own predators. These liabilities not only affect the damaged individual on a short-term basis, but also tend to reduce its overall fitness, that is, its reproductive potential. Over the long-term, fitness reduction in venom-damaged individuals results in selection against those individuals (and their genes) that tend to attack and to be envenomed by damaging stinging prey. Thus, over evolutionary time, damaging venoms select against predators lacking avoidance behavior. This is, of course, adaptive to the venomous animals not only because they are less susceptible to another attack by the particular damaged animal, but also their progeny and kin are less subjected to predatory attacks.

The damaging potential of a venom can be measured in several ways. Perhaps the most profound and precise measure of damage potential is lethal action, or the ability to kill the attacking organism. The lethalities, expressed as $LD_{50}$ (median lethal dose), of venomous hymenopterans living in the AUSD are listed in Table 5.7. The wasps and bees that are solitary, that is, live as single females rather than colonies, have venoms with $LD_{50}$ values from 76 to 12 mg/kg, values that represent only low to moderately lethal venoms. For comparison, the common honeybee, *Apis mellifera*, and the western diamondback rattlesnake, *Crotalus atrox*, have respective $LD_{50}$ values approximately 3.0 and 2.5 mg/kg (Schmidt, unpublished; Minton and Weinstein 1986). Thus, these venoms are only 4–25% as lethal as the honeybee and the rattlesnake. The venoms of the social species are much more lethal than those of the solitary species. The least lethal venom for a social species, the bumble bee *Bombus sonorus*, has the same lethality (12 mg/kg) as the most lethal solitary species. The venoms of the social wasps (Vespidae) are highly lethal and the harvester ants venoms are extraor-

Table 5.7 Lethality to mice of venoms of Hymenoptera inhabiting the AUSD

| Family | Species | LD$_{50}$ | μg Venom/ Sting | LC | References[1] |
|---|---|---|---|---|---|
| | Solitary Hymenoptera | | | | |
| Scoliidae | *Curioscolia flammicoma* >62 | | 28 | 0.4 | d |
| Pompilidae | *Pepsis formosa pattoni* | 65 | 1500 | 23 | b |
| Mutillidae | *Dasymutilla klugii* | 71 | 420 | 5.9 | a |
| Sphecidae | *Sphecius grandis* | 46 | 225 | 4.9 | d |
| Halictadae | *Nomia heteropoda* | 25 | 22 | 0.83 | d |
| Anthophoridae | *Centris pallida* | 56 | 7 | 0.13 | d |
| | *Didasia rinconis* | 76 | 7 | 0.09 | b |
| | *Habropoda pallida* | 70 | 5 | 0.07 | d |
| | *Xenoglossa angustior* | 12 | 23 | 1.9 | d |
| | *Xylocopa varipuncta* | 33 | 390 | 12 | d |
| | Social Hymenoptera | | | | |
| Apidae | *Bombus sonorus* | 12 | 760 | 62 | d |
| Vespidae | *Polistes arizonensis* | 2.0 | 180 | 90 | d |
| | *P. comanchus navajoe* | 5.0 | 200 | 40 | c |
| | *P. flavis* | 3.8 | 240 | 63 | d |
| Formicidae | *Pogonomyrmex apache* | 0.67 | 15 | 22 | d |
| | *P. barbatus* | 0.39 | 32 | 82 | d |
| | *P. bicolor* | 0.18 | 22 | 120 | d |
| | *P. desertorum* | 0.66 | 11 | 17 | d |
| | *P. rugosus* | 0.78 | 31 | 40 | d |
| | *P. californicus* | 0.60 | 20 | 33 | d |
| | *P. magnacanthus* | 0.71 | 8 | 11 | d |

[1]a = Schmidt, Blum, and Overal 1980; b = Schmidt 1986a; c = Schmidt 1983; d = Schmidt et al. unpublished.

dinarily lethal. In fact, the venoms of the harvester ants represent the most lethal known arthropod venoms.

Why the differences between the lethalities of venoms of solitary and social Hymenoptera? Although direct experimental evidence is not readily obtainable on this subject, the difference almost certainly is the result of historical and current predatory attempts by vertebrate predators. None of the solitary Hymenoptera has a large nest containing a large amount of brood or nutrition; rather, solitary Hymenoptera have small nests containing only a few cells and provisions or progeny. These nests do not constitute much of a nutritional reward to large predators and are unlikely to be attacked or require defending by the solitary nest-builder. Social species, on the other hand, live in large colonies containing large quantities of nutritious brood and/or provisions (bumble bees). These colonies provide a substantial reward to a potential predator. Thus, the selection pressure by large predators on social Hymenoptera is great, and the evolution of highly lethal venoms to deter the large predators has occurred.

Simple measurement of $LD_{50}$ does not provide a complete measure of the defensive value of a venom. The action of a venom on a predator is the product of the quantity of venom and its activity concentration (lethality). This product I have given the name lethal capacity, or LC. LC represents a more realistic indication of the tissue-damaging value of an envenomation. In Table 5.7 are listed both the amount of venom produced by an individual stinging hymenopteran and its LC. LC is the weight of predator that will receive a median lethal dose of venom from one sting. For example, only 0.4 g of mouse would have a 50% chance of dying as a result of a sting by *Curioscolia* whereas 120 g of mouse (approximately six mice) would have a 50% chance of dying from a sting by *Pogonomyrmex bicolor*. As can be seen in Table 5.7 the trend is for the venoms of the solitary species to be not very threatening to predators relative to those of the social species. The two solitary species with the greatest LC values are interesting examples of species that are midway between the two groups. Both the tarantula hawk (*Pepsis*) and the carpenter bee (*Xylocopa*) are huge shiny blue-black insects that, in themselves, represent a sizable nutritional reward. In addition, *Xylocopa varipuncta* usually communally nest in wood, and any predator that could attack the communal home would be richly rewarded. The same principle of venom LC being governed by nutritional biomass reward that must be defended applies to the social hymenopteran, *Pogonomyrmex magnacanthus*, that has the least LC value. *P. magnacanthus* is the smallest of the harvester ants in the subgenus *Pogonomyrmex* and lives in small colonies. It therefore offers the least reward for a predator.

In addition to possessing more lethal venoms, social insects have several other defensive advantages over solitary species. The most important is probably the ability to attack en masse. This not only means that the net effect is the combined total of the venoms from all stinging individuals, but it also means that each defender stands a greater chance of not being noticed by the predator during the mayhem that ensues during an attack. Unnoticed attackers are more likely to be successful in stinging a predator than those that are noticed. Other advantages include more individuals to detect an intruding potential predator and the ability to rapidly mobilize by use of pheromones other individuals to the defense.

Other forms of damage a venom can inflict on a potential predator include hemorrhagic tissue damage, blood hemolysis, tissue necrosis, and nephrotoxicity. Hemorrhagic damage is particularly common as a result of rattlesnake and lizard bites. Necrosis is sometimes observed in spider bites, and nephrotoxicity is observed in cases of mass envenomation by social wasps (Shilkin, Chen, and Khoo 1972; Hoh, Soong, and Cheng 1966; Chugh, Sharma, and Singhel 1976). Hemolysis occurs in many venoms (Schmidt, Blum, and Overal 1984). All of these damaging activities are of defensive value against vertebrate predators: they cause impairment of movement and bodily function, and in the extreme, death (infection from hemorrhagic or necrotic damage, kidney failure from nephrotoxins, and oxygen transport impairment as well as kidney blockage by hemolized blood cells).

Finally, venoms can have defensive value against large predators in three ways unrelated to those described above. These are injury by secondary infection at the sting site, noisome taste, and allergy. At first it might appear that these are incidental to envenomation, but this need not be the case. Secondary infection in lizard bites is especially important and results from microorganisms introduced during the biting process. Secondary infection of insect stings usually results from the stung animal scratching the sting site. Perhaps this sting-induced itching is partially the result of selection pressure. Probably more important than its potential value in promoting infection, itch production is beneficial to the venomous animal because it serves as a reminder to the envenomed predator that it was stung and hurt by the insect it had attacked.

Some venoms are active topical allomones when applied to moist tissues such as inside the mouth. For example, the venoms of *Odontomachus desertorum, Bombus sonorus,* and *Xylocopa varipuncta* are very bitter tasting, and those of *Pogonomyrmex rugosus* and *X. varipuncta* taste hydrolytic or corrosive and leave a burning sensation in the mouth (author's personal observations). Such responses are likely to be effective deterrents against some predators as, for example, the refusal of red-winged blackbirds (*Agelaius phoeniceus*) to eat additional bumble bees after eating the middle (venom-containing) segments of the abdomen of a bee (Evans and Waldbauer 1982).

The ability to produce allergic reactions in stung predators is of distinctive advantage to a venomous prey. Allergic reactions (anaphylaxis and the like) are very terrifying to the envenomed animal or person (see Schmidt 1986b for discussion) as well as debilitating and potentially life threatening. All of these reactions are of defensive value. Fright might prevent the animal from attacking the venomous animal again or others within its population (who are likely to be kin). The damaging effects reduce the predator's food collecting abilities and possibly its survival. Definitive data pertaining to the evolutionary reasons, if any, as to why venoms are allergenic are virtually impossible to obtain. By inference, however, the fact that hymenopterous venoms cause severe allergic reactions much more frequently than do other materials is not inconsistent with an interpretation that selection pressure by predators has favored insect venoms that are more allergenic.

Individual defensive attributes of venoms cannot be considered simply in isolation. The various properties act in synergism to produce a much greater effect than any one activity or arithmetic sum of activities alone. The synergism of venom components to produce enhanced pharmacological activities is well documented (that is, phospholipase $A_2$ and melittin in the honeybee [Vogt et al. 1970]; phospholipase and crotoxin in elapid snakes [Louv and Visser 1978]). Similar synergism occurs at the higher level of defense itself. For example, pain and toxic effects enhance each other's effects. The pain gets the immediate attention of the envenomed predator, but if this is short-lived and not followed by other effects, the predator can quickly learn to ignore it. Swelling, debility, damage-induced pain, and/or sickness that result from one or more stings take time to become evident and alone would only produce delayed antipredator deterrence. Together the two effects can act to stop the immediate attack and then later to punish the attacker. The combination serves as a great "truthful" message to the predator that real danger exists in attacking that venomous prey. Other combinations of actions, for example, pain and allergic anaphylaxis or noisome taste and venom-damaged tissue swelling, will yield similar enhanced defensive activity.


## CONCLUSIONS

The Arizona Upland Sonoran Desert is a small region in the United States and Mexico that contains an abundance of spiny and thorny plants and venomous animals. These adaptations are of defensive value against large vertebrate herbivores and predators. Spines help defend against vertebrates by causing tissue damage in several ways: punctures, rips or tears, barbs that often cause spine retention in the flesh, venoms, and infections. Animal venoms have defensive value against vertebrates via the induction of pain, tissue damage, topical allomonal activity, infection, and possibly allergy.


## ACKNOWLEDGMENTS

I am indebted to many people for information and provocative discussions relating to this subject. Taxonomic help from David Sissom, Stanley Williams, Roland Shelley, Karen Reichard, Mark Dimmitt, and Becky and Tom Van Devender was greatly appreciated. I am grateful to Stephen

Buchmann, Janice Bowers, David Evans, Douglas Whitman, Tony Burgess, Ray Turner, Carl Olson, Pat Schmidt, and Paul Martin for manuscript reviews.

## REFERENCES

Bernstein, I. L., Sigmundi, R. A. 1980. Tumor anorexia: a learned food aversion? *Science* 209:416–18.

Bowers, J. E. 1980. Flora of Organ Pipe Cactus National Monument. *J. Ariz.-Nev. Acad. Sci.* 15:1–11, 33–47.

Bowers, J. E., McLaughlin, S. P. 1987. Flora and vegetation of the Rincon Mountains, Pima County, Arizona. *Desert Plants* 8:51–94.

Chugh, K. S., Sharma, B. K., Singhal, P. C. 1976. Acute renal failure following hornet stings. *J. Trop. Med. Hyg.* 79:42–44.

Conant, R. 1958. *A Field Guide to Reptiles and Amphibians*. Boston: Houghton Mifflin. 366 pp.

Creighton, W. S. 1950. The ants of North America. *Bull. Mus. Comp. Zool. (Harvard)* 104:1–585.

Delgado Quiroz, A. 1978. Venoms of Lepidoptera. In *Handbook of Experimental Pharmacology*. Vol. 48 Arthropod Venoms. Ed. S. Bettini, 555–611. Berlin: Springer-Verlag. 997 pp.

Erspamer, V., Erspamer, G. F., Mazzanti, G., Endean, R. 1984. Active peptides in the skin of one hundred amphibian species from Australia and Papua New Guinea. *Comp. Biochem. Physiol.* 77(C): 99–108.

Evans, D. L., Waldbauer, G. P. 1982. Behavior of adult and naive birds when presented with a bumble bee and its mimic. *Z. Tiepsychologie* 59:247–59.

Flier, J., Edwards, M. W., Daly, J. W., Meyers, C. W. 1980. Widespread occurrence in frogs and toads of skin compounds interacting with the ouabain site of Na +, K$^+$-ATPase. *Science* 208:503–5.

Gertsch, W. J., Ennik, F. 1983. The spider genus *Loxosceles* in North America, Central America, and the West Indies (Araneae, Loxoscelidae). *Bull. Am. Mus. Nat. Hist.* 175:264–360.

Glenn, J. L., Straight, R. C. 1982. The rattlesnakes and their venom yield and lethal toxicity. In *Rattlesnake Venoms: Their Action and Treatment*. Ed. A. T. Tu, 3–119. New York: Marcel Dekker. 393 pp.

Goldberg, D. E., Turner, R. M. 1986. Vegetation change and plant demography in permanent plots in the Sonoran Desert. *Ecology* 67:695–712.

Hoh, T. K., Soong, C. L., Cheng, C. T. 1966. Fatal haemolysis from wasp and hornet sting. *Singapore Med. J.* 7:122–26.

Islam, S. 1979. Severe conditioned taste aversion elicited by venom of Russell's viper. *Experientia* 35:1206–7.

Janzen, D. H. 1966. Coevolution of mutualism between ants and acacias in Central America. *Evolution* 20:249–75.

Kearney, T. H., Peebles, R. H. 1960. *Arizona Flora*. Berkeley: University of California Press. 1085 pp.

Krombein, K. V., Hurd, P. D., Jr., Smith, D. R., Burks, B. D. 1979. *Catalog of Hymenoptera in America North of Mexico*. Vol. 2, 1199–2209. Washington, D.C.: Smithsonian.

Lane, M. A. 1981. Vegetation and flora of McDowell Mountain Regional Park, Maricopa County, Arizona. *J. Ariz.-Nev. Acad. Sci.* 16:29–38.

Louw, A. I., Visser, L. 1978. The synergism of cardiotoxin and phospholipase A₂ in hemolysis. *Biochim. Biophys. Acta* 512:163–71.

Lowe, C. H., Schwalbe, C. R., Johnson, T. B. 1986. *The Venomous Reptiles of Arizona*. Phoenix: Arizona Game and Fish Department. 115 pp.

Mickel, C. E. 1928. Biological and taxonomic investigations on the mutillid wasps. *Bull. U.S. Nat. Mus.* 143:1–351.

———. 1935. Descriptions and records of nearctic mutillid wasps of the genera *Myrmilloides* and *Pseudomethoca*. *Trans. Am. Entomol. Soc.* 61:383–98.

Minelli, A. 1978. Secretions of centipedes. *See* Delgado Quiroz (1978), 72–85.

Minton, S. A., Weinstein, S. A. 1986. Geographic and ontogenic variation in venom of the western diamondback rattlesnake (*Crotalus atrox*). *Toxicon* 24:71–80.

Russell, F. E. 1986. A confusion of spiders. *Emergency Med.* 18(11): 8–9, 13.

Russell, F. E., Gertsch, W. J. 1983. Letter to the editor. *Toxicon* 21:337–39.

Schmidt, J. O. 1982. Biochemistry of insect venoms. *Ann. Rev. Entomol.* 27:339–68.

———. 1983. Hymenopteran envenomation. In *Urban Entomology: Interdisciplinary Perspectives*. Eds. G. W. Frankie, C. S. Koehler, 187–220. New York: Praeger. 493 pp.

———. 1986a. Chemistry, pharmacology, and chemical ecology of ant venoms. In *Venoms of the Hymenoptera*. Ed. T. Piek, 425–508. London: Academic. 570 pp.

———. 1986b. Allergy to Hymenoptera venoms. *See* Schmidt (1986a), 509–46.

Schmidt, J. O., Blum, M. S. 1977. Adaptations and responses of *Dasymutilla occidentalis* (Hymenoptera: Mutillidae) to predators. *Entomol. Exp. Appl.* 21:99–111.

———. 1979. Toxicity of *Dolichovespula maculata* venom. *Toxicon* 17:645–48.

Schmidt, J. O., Blum, M. S., Overal, W. L. 1980. Comparative lethality of venoms from stinging Hymenoptera. *Toxicon* 18:469–74.

———. 1984. Hemolytic activities of stinging insect venoms. *Arch. Insect Biochem. Physiol.* 1:155–60.

———. 1986. Comparative enzymology of venoms from stinging Hymenoptera. *Toxicon* 24:907–21.

Schmidt, J. O., Yamane, S., Matsuura, M., Starr, C. K. 1986. Hornet venoms: lethalities and lethal capacities. *Toxicon* 24:950–54.

Shilkin, K. B., Chen, B. T. M., Khoo, O. T. 1972. Rhabdomyolysis caused by hornet venom. *Br. Med. J.* 1:156–57.

Starr, C. K. 1985. A simple pain scale for field comparison of hymenopteran stings. *J. Entomol. Sci.* 20:225–32.

Stebbins, R. C. 1985. *A Field Guide to Western Reptiles and Amphibians*. 2d ed. Boston: Houghton Mifflin. 336 pp.

Turner, R. M., Brown, D. E. 1982. Sonoran desertscrub. *Desert Plants* 4:180–221.

Vogt, W., Patzer, P., Lege, L., Oldigs, H.-D., Wille, G. 1970. Synergism between phospholipase A and various peptides and SH-reagents in causing haemolysis. *Naunyn-Schmiedebergs Arch. Pharmakol. Exp. Pathol.* 265:442–54.

Whittaker, R. H. 1956. Vegetation of the Great Smoky Mountains. *Ecol. Monog.* 26:1–80.

———. 1960. Vegetation of the Siskiyou Mountains, Oregon and California. *Ecol. Monog.* 30:279–338.

Whittaker, R. H., Niering, W. A. 1965. Vegetation of the Santa Catalina Mountains, Arizona: a gradient analysis of the south slope. *Ecology* 46:429–52.

———. 1968. Vegetation of the Santa Catalina Mountains, Arizona III species distribution and floristic relations on the north slope. *J. Ariz. Acad. Sci.* 5:3–21.

# 6

# BIOLOGICAL AND SOCIAL REPERCUSSIONS OF IRRIGATED PECAN AGRICULTURE IN SOUTHERN ARIZONA

Kenneth J. Kingsley

University of Arizona
Tucson, Arizona

## INTRODUCTION

Riparian habitat was once a characteristic and important part of the Southwest. The history of the Santa Cruz River, as described by Johnson and Carothers (1982), was typical of desert rivers. The Santa Cruz River runs northward from Mexico through southern Arizona eventually joining the Gila River about 10 km south of Phoenix. Phillips, Marshall, and Monson (1964) describe a portion of the river: "Prior to World War II, the [Santa Cruz] river at Sahuarita Butte was a paradise for birds. There were fine groves of cottonwoods, and, in the more open areas, thickets of batamote, *Baccharis glutinosa*, on the sandy bottoms back of the shallow channel itself. Along the irrigation ditch and elsewhere grew tree tobacco. Above these bottoms was a dense but not tall mesquite thicket, of a general level of fifteen feet or more, with much understory of vines and flowers in the summer rainy season." Native riparian habitat has been lauded as the most valuable wildlife habitat in the arid Southwest, possibly the most valuable in North America. Several species of birds, such as the yellow-billed cuckoo, blue grosbeak, yellow warbler, black phoebe, lazuli bunting, and many others are characteristically found only in riparian habitat (Monson and Phillips 1981). Some species depend on riparian habitats only during certain seasons, whereas others require such habitats for their entire lives. Populations of these birds appear to be generally declining as native riparian habitat disappears (Gaines 1977). Several symposia and numerous scientific papers have addressed the wildlife, aesthetic, and recreational values of native riparian habitats and lamented their rapid decline (Johnson et al. 1985; Warner and Hendrix 1984; Johnson and Carothers 1982; Johnson and McCormick 1978; Johnson and Jones 1977; Sands 1977). The original extent of riparian habitat is poorly documented and that which remains is inadequately defined (Johnson and Carothers 1982). There have been estimates that we have lost from 90 to 95% of our native habitat (Johnson and Carothers 1982).

Riparian habitat has been destroyed by a combination of factors, summarized by Johnson and Carothers (1982). Overgrazing has damaged the watersheds, causing rapid runoff and flooding rather than gentle seepage into rivers. Repeated flooding carries sand and soil from place to place, changing the flood plain and filling the river channel. Pumping underground water for agricultural, mining, municipal, and industrial uses has lowered water tables. Water impoundments, flood control schemes, and phreatophyte control have contributed to reshaping flow regimes and habitat characteristics of watercourses. Firewood cutting has eliminated most of the mesquite forests. This overall elimination of habitat has greatly affected the wildlife that depends upon it.

Agricultural development has also had profound effects on riparian habitat, but these have been little documented (Conine et al. 1978; Kingsley 1985a; Ohmart, Anderson, and Hunter 1985; Wells, Anderson, and Ohmart 1979). Habitats may improve for some species and deteriorate for others. Ohmart, Anderson, and Hunter (1985) found that agriculture created new habitats for wading, water, and shorebirds, and that the type of agricultural development and the types of crop grown were important in determining species composition and population sizes. Conine et al. (1978) found that some riparian species used agricultural land as foraging habitat, whereas other species did not. Again, type of agricultural development and type of crop were important in determining habitat use by birds. Wells, Anderson, and Ohmart (1979) examined avian use of citrus orchards and found that citrus was an important habitat for doves, but generally lacked flycatchers, small insectivores, and woodpeckers which were abundant in native riparian habitat. Kingsley (1985a) listed 66 species of birds utilizing pecan orchards, including several that are characteristically found in native riparian habitats. These included a number of flycatchers and small insectivores. Woodpeckers were not found nesting in the orchard but were frequently seen foraging in it. Many other vertebrate taxa found in native riparian habitat were also found in the pecan orchards. That list has increased in the present paper by several additional species observed in the past year.

Irrigated agriculture has flourished in the Santa Cruz Valley for hundreds of years. Native American farmers were replaced by the Spanish who were in turn replaced by Anglos. All practiced the same basic flood irrigation techniques and grew some of the same crops, primarily cotton. It is the scale of agriculture that has changed greatly over time. In the 1950s, the Sahuarita–Green Valley area had more than 2,450 ha of cotton and small grains (K. Walden, personal communication). A few mesquite trees remained in places along the river banks, but essentially the native riparian habitat was gone, along with its native animals that require riparian habitat.

The pecan tree, *Carya illinoensis* Koch, is a native of the southern United States and northern Mexico. Wild pecans are found from west central Texas to western Alabama in the east and extend up the Mississippi River and its tributaries into southern Illinois (Wolstenholme 1979). In its native range the pecan tree is largely confined to bottomlands and flood plains bordering rivers and streams. In prime habitat, the wild pecan is so successful as a competitor that virtually all other significant tree species are eliminated. Native pecans tend to grow best in areas that occasionally flood (Wolstenholme 1979). With the exception of one paper on wildlife pest control in pecans (Couch 1981), studies of native pecan stands as wildlife habitat are not known.

Pecans are not native in Arizona, but were introduced in about 1920 (Mielke and True 1981). In 1983, 6,680 commercial ha of pecan trees were grown in Arizona, mostly in Pima, Pinal, and Maricopa counties (Hathorn 1984). All pecan culture in Arizona depends upon irrigation. Drip irrigation has been used successfully on some of the smaller plantings of pecans (Bach and Kuykendall 1971), but the largest orchards use flooded border irrigation (D. Fangmeier, personal communication) with one 2,200 ha farm annually pumping about 40,249,440 $m^3$ of water (K. Walden, personal communication).

The farm contains rows of trees surrounded by borders 10 m wide and up to 300 m long. Borders are filled with water to a depth of from 10 to 15 cm. Each day sections of different fields are irrigated, with a complete rotation around the farm approximately every two weeks. Irrigation efficiency is highly variable, depending to a large degree on weather, microhabitat, and soil type. Dense shade provided by the trees probably helps reduce evaporation. During the drier parts of the year, water percolates through the soil rather quickly, but the soils on approximately 20% of the farm contain enough clay that puddles may last for several days to a week. Improvement of soils by addition of gypsum and other amendments has been attempted. During the rainy season in July and August, parts of some fields may remain wet continuously, creating a swamp that may last for several weeks. Dense weeds may grow in this wet soil. Figure 6.1 shows a typical flooded border in a pecan field.

Figure 6.1.   Typical flooded border between rows of pecan
trees. Photographed immediately following irrigation.

The trees were originally planted at a density of 237 trees per ha on
1,012 ha, 198 trees per ha on 405 ha, and 119 trees per ha on 1,012 ha.
Thinning has occurred on most of the land, so that present tree density
does not exceed 119 trees per ha, and in the fields with the largest trees,
density is now 59 trees per ha. Eventually a density of 30 trees per ha is
anticipated (Walden 1970). With the exception of trees planted to replace
the very few that have died, all trees in a given field are of the same age
and very similar in size. Dead trees and dead branches are promptly
removed, eliminating snags which may be important bird habitat in native
habitats (Miller and Miller 1980). Tree holes caused by rot setting in where
branches have broken off apparently do not occur because the trees are
well cared for and broken limbs treated to prevent infection by *Cytospora*
sp., a native fungus.

A permanent shrub midstory is not present and would not be tolerated
in the orchard. However, sprout regrowth from stumps occurs irregularly
and may function as a shrub midstory in providing habitat. Song sparrows
and Abert's towhees, both characteristically found in dense undergrowth
in riparian situations (Monson and Phillips 1981), nest in the sprouts. A

structural approximation of a shrub midstory is created around the edges
of many fields by slash piles, where prunings from the trees are dumped
(Figure 6.2). The slash is not burned because of Pima County Health Department rules relating to possible air pollution. Several wildlife species utilize the slash piles as shelter. Rock squirrels, *Spermophilus variegatus* Hall
and Kelson, abundant agricultural pests on the farm, build burrows under
the slash piles. Abert's towhees and song sparrows also can occasionally
be found in these piles. Red-winged blackbirds, Brewer's blackbirds, yellow-
headed blackbirds, and Gambel's quail roost in the slash piles.

The farm is, for much of its extent, adjacent to or very near urban development. The southern half of the farm has had the land on the west side of
the Santa Cruz River developed as the Green Valley retirement community. Green Valley presently is a thriving retirement community of approximately 15,000 residents. It is rapidly growing, with projections for a
population of approximately 50,000 residents by the year 2000. Much of
the development will be on land that is presently in pecans. The development grew up on the west side of the orchard, paralleling the orchard and
the river. Between the orchard and the houses, in the area designated as

Figure 6.2.    Slash pile adjacent to orchard.

flood plain, golf courses and recreation centers were created. Developmental plans call for more golf courses in some of the flood plain, with about 850 ha remaining in pecans indefinitely. On the northern half of the farm, adjacent to the orchard at widely scattered locations are individual houses, the community of Sahuarita, and a trailer park.

Over the years, the pecan trees on the farm have grown and appear to be maturing into a biotic community very similar to native riparian community in some ways, yet also quite different from it. This paper describes the environment of the farm and its faunal components. These observations were made incidental to a study of insect pests in the orchard.

## BIOLOGICAL REPERCUSSIONS

### Agricultural Pests and Their Management

*INSECT PESTS.*   The most important agricultural pests, in terms of influence on pecan production, are the blackmargined aphid, *Monellia caryella* (Fitch) and the black pecan aphid, *Melanocallis caryaefoliae* (Davis). Populations of aphids are closely monitored by regular sampling, and when populations appear to be increasing, control measures are instituted. Traditionally, aphid control has been attempted through use of insecticidal sprays. The growers recognize the potential dangers that may result from overuse of chemical insecticides, such as the possibilities of development of resistant pest populations, adverse impact on beneficial species, and secondary pest outbreaks. A program of research and development of integrated pest management strategies is supported by the growers. The value of beneficial insects (predators) has not been determined in pecans, and there have been no documented instances of pecan insects developing resistance to insecticides (Harris 1983). Based upon their experience with other crops, however, the growers maintain their concern about overuse of pesticides. An additional complication is created by the proximity of the orchard to urban development. Some urban residents are concerned about the possibility of contamination of their environment with chemical pesticides. The growers have selected the chemicals they use with these considerations in mind. To reduce the likelihood of development of resistant pest populations, no chemical insecticide is used consistently for more than two years. After using one chemical insecticide for one or two seasons, another is selected that differs in chemistry and mode of action. This results in a constant search for alternatives.

The second most important pest does not feed on pecan trees, but creates an extremely complex problem for the growers. Enormous numbers of floodwater mosquitoes, *Aedes vexans* (Meigen) and *Psorophora columbiae* (Dyar and Knab), breed in the orchard. The bionomics and management of these species are discussed extensively in Kingsley (1985b). These species are migratory, attack in swarms, and are fierce, persistent, noisy, and painful biters. Before an effective management program had been developed, bite counts in the orchard commonly exceeded 50 per minute at mid-day. Dozens of complaints each year were made by nearby residents to the Pima County Health Department, and political tensions were mounting. Traditionally, after several complaints had been received, the County Health Department would notify the growers, who would spray the orchard with a chemical insecticide, generally the chemical that they were currently using for aphid control. This resulted in the temporary suppression of the population of adult mosquitoes. However, eggs deposited in the soil by adult mosquitoes would hatch with the next irrigation, and a new generation of mosquitoes would be produced. Because portions of the orchard were continually being irrigated, hordes of mosquitoes were continually being produced. No one was satisfied with this approach to the problem. The growers expressed serious concern about overuse of chemical insecticides for mosquito control. They feared that overuse might complicate their aphid control program by killing beneficial insects as well as increase the probability of the aphids developing resistance to the chemicals.

A system of management of mosquito populations was developed through research, with the support of the growers and Zoecon Corportion (Kingsley 1985b). Water management, ground leveling, and soil improvement are components of the management program, but the most important component is use of the bacterium *Bacillus thuringiensis israelensis (B.t.i.)*. *B.t.i.* is a naturally occurring strain of a common soil bacterium which was discovered to be highly toxic when ingested by mosquito larvae (Margalit and Dean 1985). The primary challenge in utilizing *B.t.i.* for mosquito management is in the development of strategies and systems for the delivery of the material to the organisms at effective dose rates (McLaughlin and Vidrine 1984) at reasonable costs (Legner and Sjogren 1984). The system uses *B.t.i.* (Zoecon's product Teknar R HPO) dripped into irrigation water at or near the wells at the rate of 1.5–2 ppm product to water for 4 hours beginning approximately 12 hours after the start of irrigation. This is followed by spray application of a 1 part product to 64 parts water to puddles at the downstream ends of irrigation borders, two to three days following irrigation. Adjustment of dose rates may be temporarily necessary to combat seasonal peaks of the mosquito population. This program has been very effective in reducing mosquito populations. No complaints have been made by local residents during the two seasons that the program has been implemented, and field personnel are no longer plagued by mosquitoes. The growers believe that the program is cost-effective and reasonable. Research continues into better methods of mosquito management in this situation, including the use of alternative control measures to reduce the probability of development of *B.t.i.*-resistant populations.

No other insect pests are considered to be important in this orchard at this time. Although many species of insects feed on native pecan trees, few are really considered important pests. The potential pest complex has evolved in the presence of a complex of natural enemies (Harris 1983). Pecan pests, in general, are highly localized in distribution through the areas of the world in which pecans are cultivated (Harris 1983). That there are so few in this area may indicate that they just have not been brought to the area yet.

*VERTEBRATE PESTS.*   The most important vertebrate pest is the rock squirrel, *Spermophilus variegatus* Hall and Kelson. Large numbers of rock squirrels inhabit the slash piles around the periphery of the farm, and some build burrows in ditch banks and other suitable locations. No study has been attempted of the economic impact of the squirrels, but the growers estimate that squirrels consume about $100,000 worth of nuts each year. Squirrels may also damage trees by stripping bark, which may be more costly over time (Mullenax, Polles, and Gibson 1984). In some pecan-growing areas, squirrels may be responsible for as much as a one-third reduction in pecan yield (Mullenax, Polles, and Gibson 1984). Attempts to manage the squirrel population include protection of natural enemies such as hawks and coyotes and shooting. Coyotes and raptors are common in the orchard, but appear to be generally ineffective in lowering the squirrel population. The slash piles are sufficiently dense to be good protective cover. I have frequently observed squirrels perched on branches in slash piles giving alarm calls as raptors fly overhead. Squirrels are most vulnerable when they are crossing roads between slash piles and pecan trees.

The squirrel population was drastically reduced by a major flood in October 1983. Although no records were kept, few squirrels were seen from the time immediately following the flood until the spring of 1985, when they became very abundant again. This suggests that the squirrel population is extremely resilient and can build quickly following drastic losses. It may be in the grower's interest to support a study that would examine the actual economic impact of rock squirrels on the crop and develop a management plan for squirrels. A more effective management plan should consider the possibility of increasing populations of natural enemies of squirrels on the property and habitat modification by removing slash piles.

Although the possiblity may seem remote, the potential of the squirrel population being involved in transmission of plague to humans should be considered. The rock squirrel is an important amplifying host of plague

(Olkowski and Daar 1985), and a large population of squirrels near human habitation is a potentially serious situation, should plague ever become established in the squirrels. Cases of plague are apparently increasing, particularly in situations where human use of areas with large rodent populations is increasing, such as new urban development in formerly undeveloped land (Olkowski and Daar 1985). Management of the rock squirrel population might not only reduce the economic loss to the pecan growers, but might also avoid a potential public health problem.

Pocket gophers, *Thomomys bottae* (Eydoux and Gervais), are generally rare in the orchard, and are found only around its periphery. Apparently, gophers invade from land around the orchard, but are unable to become well established in the irrigated area, probably because they are unable to tolerate frequent flooding. The growers express some concern about loss of irrigation water through gopher burrows and attempt to control gophers when burrows are found.

Raccoons, *Procyon lotor* (L.), are mentioned in the literature as being pecan pests (Brison 1974, Mullenax, Polles, and Gibson 1984) that consume nuts. In this orchard raccoon tracks are fairly common, but it is unknown whether these animals are consuming pecans in economically important amounts.

Ravens, both the common raven *Corvus corax* and the Chihuahuan raven *Corvus cryptoleucus*, are abundant pests consuming ripe pecans during the autumn. No attempt has been made to estimate the economic impact of ravens, and no attempts have been made to manage raven depredation on the crop. In the context of the large scale of this pecan operation, the overall impact of ravens is probably slight. In smaller pecan plantations, depredation by the American crow, *Corvus brachyrhynchos* Brehm, may be extremely serious (Couch 1981; Brison 1974), but the literature makes no mention of ravens. Crows are not present in the study area, but ravens may be the ecological equivalent of crows in this context. In the long-term management plan for the orchard, which calls for considerable reduction in land used for pecans, it is possible that the impact of ravens may increase proportionally with the decrease in number of trees.

WEEDS. The growers attempt to control weeds by mowing. It is important to the harvesting technique to have a good bed of turf under the trees wherever possible (K. Walden, personal communication). Most of the plants that provide this turf are weeds, so elimination of the plants by herbicides would be detrimental to the overall operation. Mowing is occasionally supplemented by careful use of herbicides in restricted locations for particularly troublesome weed problems. During the rainy season in July and August some fields become too muddy to permit mowing, and dense thickets of weeds grow in some borders. The dominant weed species is barnyard grass, *Echinochloa cruzgalli* (L.) Beauv., which can grow to more than two meters in height. Other important weed species include Bermudagrass, *Cynodon dactylon* (L.) Pers., yellow nutsedge, *Cyperus esculentus* L., and *Amaranthus* spp. All of these are potentially important producers of forage for wildlife (Martin, Zim, and Nelson 1951). Weeds also provide roosting harborage for mosquitoes and may also provide food for adult mosquitoes. Mosquito bite counts were always lower in weed-free fields. Careful weed management is an important component of the management programs for both water and mosquitoes.

## Beneficial and Neutral Species

*INVERTEBRATES.* Probably the most important and conspicuous beneficial insects in the orchard are aphid predators and parasites and dragonflies which are predators on mosquitoes. Leser (1981) found three species of coccinellids, the lacewings *Chrysopa carnea* Stephens and *Hemerobius* sp., syrphid larvae, several species of spiders, assassin bugs, *Sinea* sp. and *Zelus* sp., bigeyed bugs, *Geocoris* sp., and damsel bugs, *Nabis* sp., as predators on *Monellia caryella*. He also found a parasitoid wasp, *Aphelinus perpallidus* Gahan, which attacked over 50% of the aphids during the aphid population peak. He concluded, however, that there was no indication that the parasites or predators he observed were important factors limiting aphid population increases. Harris (1983) pointed out that the value of conservation of natural enemies of pecan pests has not been demonstrated, but that such conservation through elimination of unnecessary pesticide treatments may be important.

Several species of mosquito predators are present in the orchard. Dragonflies are generally recognized as predators on mosquitoes, but they cannot be relied upon to decrease mosquito populations markedly (Hinman 1934b). This is because they are opportunistic feeders, feeding where their prey is already abundant and switching to alternate prey easily (Corbet 1980). At least nine species of dragonflies have been found in the orchard. The amount of permanent water suitable for breeding habitat for dragonflies seems insufficient in the area to support the large dragonfly population. Dragonfly larvae require long-lasting water (Corbet 1980), and the only water present in the immediate vicinity that seems suitable is in cowponds and golf course water hazards, which are stocked with fish that might eat or compete with dragonfly larvae. I have found a few dragonfly larvae in some irrigation ditches. Adults are frequently seen ovipositing in ditches and flooded borders, but I have not found water in the orchard that remains long enough for dragonfly larvae to grow to maturity.

The hydrophilid beetles *Hydrophilus triangularis* Say and *Tropisternus lateralis* (F.) are common in the orchard. Several species of Notonectidae are also common in flooded borders. Apparently all of these aquatic species are immigrants, rapidly invading flooded borders and ditches and unsuccessfully attempting to reproduce.

Many species of insects are predators on mosquito larvae, but the impact on mosquito populations is not clear and may be highly variable (Hinman 1934a). James (1964) found that in some instances aquatic Coleoptera can be important in regulating mosquito populations. Zalom and Grigarick (1980) found that *Hydrophilus triangularis* and *Tropisternus lateralis* had no effect on mosquito populations in California rice fields. Miura, Takahashi, and Mulligan (1978) found that predator insects, especially notonectids, were important in controlling populations of *Culex tarsalis* Coquillett in experimental ponds which held permanent water. In the orchard situation, with transitory water and rapidly developing mosquitoes, it is unlikely that predators alone could effectively keep the mosquito population below a level that resulted in no annoyance to people (Kingsley 1985b). Natural enemies may be of some value, however, and the mosquito control strategy used conserves natural enemies. Mulligan and Schaefer (1981) showed that *B.t.i.* integrated well with natural predators. Treatment with *B.t.i.* had no detrimental effect on the predators, but reduced the prey population to a level that made subsequent control of mosquitoes by predators effective.

Many neutral species of invertebrates are abundant in the orchard, but they have not been investigated. A systematic survey of the invertebrates of the orchard would probably turn up many taxa that are characteristically found in native riparian or aquatic habitats.

*VERTEBRATES.* The vertebrate fauna is more conspicuous and easier to note with casual observation than the invertebrates. Birds are the only vertebrates for which I have kept consistent records, the other vertebrates being observed incidentally during my other studies.

*Fish.* Only one species of fish, *Gambusia affinis* (Baird and Girard), is found in the orchard. These fish were planted in livestock watering ponds adjacent to the orchard, one of which is filled by an irrigation canal. Occasionally some fish swim upstream and get out of the canal into the borders when irrigation is occurring. They live for a few days and then die when the water dries up.

*Amphibians.* Several species of toads are abundant in the orchard. The Colorado River toad, *Bufo alvarius* Girard, breeds in the ditches and also in some of the waterlogged borders. Red spotted toads, *Bufo punctatus* Baird and Girard, and Great Plains toads, *Bufo cognatus* Say, are abundant and breed successfully in some of the borders, although most of the tadpoles are stranded when the irrigation water seeps into the soil. Early in irrigation season, most of the amphibians' reproductive effort is wasted, since water does not remain long enough for tadpoles to mature. Once the summer rains have begun, many puddles in the orchard originally created by irrigation water are replenished by rain water and last long enough for successful toad reproduction. Couch's spadefoot toads, *Scaphiopus couchi* Baird, breed very successfully in parts of the orchard during the summer rainy season.

*Reptiles.*     Reptiles are much less common in the orchard than amphibians. Apparently the ground-living reptiles can not survive well or reproduce successfully in repeatedly inundated habitat (Warren and Schwalbe 1985). I have seen a few tree lizards, *Urosaurus ornatus* Baird and Girard, and desert spiny lizards, *Sceloporus magister* Hallowell, but lizards appear to be, at least to casual observation, rather scarce. Suitable microhabitats for many of the native lizard species (Jones and Glinski 1985) are not present in this orchard as a result of orchard management techniques.

Like lizards, snakes also are uncommon. In three summers, I have not seen a rattlesnake in the orchard, although farm workers have told me that they have seen rattlesnakes. I have seen two gopher snakes, *Pituophis melanoleucus* Daudin, and one garter snake, *Thamnophis* sp. Although the species of *Thamnophis* was not positively identified, there are only two possibilities, *T. eques* Reuss and *T. cyrtopsis* Kennicott, both of which are declining in numbers and are clearly threatened with extirpation in the Southwest due to habitat destruction (Lowe 1985). The orchard may be suitable habitat for this snake, and knowledge of the snake's biology in the orchard may be useful in protecting this declining species.

*Birds.*     Birds are abundant in the orchard. A list of the birds observed in the orchard is presented in Table 6.1. Some discussion of a few species may contribute to an understanding of the biological repercussions of the orchard.

Hawks are abundant: red-tailed hawks and Cooper's hawks are present all year, apparently feeding on rock squirrels. Other raptors are seasonally common to abundant. Most are apparently migrating through the area, discover the abundant squirrels, and stay for a few days or weeks. No raptor nests have been found in the orchard. Mechanized harvesting of pecans involves violent shaking of the trees with tree-shaking machines which might dislodge nests. Good nest sites may be a limiting factor for the raptor population. Erection of artificial nest platforms might result in an increase in raptors, which might be useful in reducing the squirrel population.

Several species of birds characteristically found in native riparian habitats have settled in the orchard. Yellow-billed cuckoos, which are scarce and declining in native habitats (Gaines 1977), appear to be abundant in the orchard. I have not attempted a systematic count, but there is approximately one nesting pair per ten acres. This is approximately the same density observed by R. R. Johnson (personal communication) in mature cottonwood forests on the Salt and Verde rivers, Arizona. Black phoebes,

Table 6.1. Birds observed in the pecan orchard. Nomenclature and order follow A.O.U. Checklist 1983. Abundance and status refer only to the orchard, not the surrounding desert and urban areas. Codes—Abundance: A = Abundant, C = Common, U = Uncommon, R = Rare; Status: V = Visitor, B = Breeds, ? = Unknown; * = Characteristically riparian habitat dependent.

Green-winged Teal *Anas crecca* RV
Turkey Vulture *Cathartes aura* CV
Osprey *Pandion haliaetus* RV
Black-shouldered Kite *Elanus caeruleus* RV
Northern Harrier *Circus cyaneus* RV
Sharp-shinned Hawk *Accipiter striatus* UV
Cooper's Hawk *Accipiter cooperi* CV
Harris' Hawk *Parabuteo unicinctus* RV
Swainson's Hawk *Buteo swainsoni* CV
Red-tailed Hawk *Buteo jamaicensis* AV
American Kestrel *Falco sparverius* CV
Peregrin Falcon *Falco peregrinus* RV
Gambel's Quail *Callipepla gambelii* AB
Killdeer *Charadrius vociferus* RV
Rock Dove *Columba livia* RV
White-winged Dove *Zenaida asiatica* AB
Mourning Dove *Zenaida macroura* AB
Inca Dove *Columbina inca* CB
Common Ground-Dove *Columbina passerina*CB
Yellow-billed Cuckoo *Coccyzus americanus*CB*
Greater Roadrunner *Geococcyx californianus*CV
Common Barn-Owl *Tyto alba* CV
Great Horned Owl *Bubo virginianus* CV
Lesser Nighthawk *Chordeiles acutipennis* CV
Common Poorwill *Phalaenoptilus nutallii* CV
Black-chinned Hummingbird
  *Archilochus alexandri* CV
Rufous Hummingbird *Selasphorus rufus* RV
Gila Woodpecker *Melanerpes uropygialis* CV
Ladder-backed Woodpecker *Picoides scalaris*CV
Northern Flicker *Colaptes auratus* CV
Western Wood-Pewee *Contopus sordidulus* RV
Black Phoebe *Sayornis nigricans* CB*
Say's Phoebe *Sayornis saya* CB
Vermilion Flycatcher *Pyrocephalus rubinus* CB*
Western Kingbird *Tyrannus verticalis* AB*
Purple Martin *Progne subis* UV
Violet-green Swallow *Tachycineta thalassina* UV
Northern Rough-winged Swallow
  *Stelgidopteryx serripennis* UV
Chihuahuan Raven *Corvus cryptoleucus* CV
Common Raven *Corvus corax* AV
Verdin *Auriparus flaviceps* UV
Cactus Wren
  *Campylorhynchus brunneicapillus* CV

Bewick's Wren *Thryomanes bewickii* U?
Ruby-crowned Kinglet *Regulus calendula* UV
American Robin *Turdus migratorius* UV
Northern Mockingbird *Mimus polyglottos* UV
Curve-billed Thrasher *Toxostoma curvirostre* UV
Water Pipit *Anthus spinoletta* UV
Phainopepla *Phainopepla nitens* RV
Loggerhead Shrike *Lanius ludovicianus* RV
European Starling *Sturnus vulgaris* AV
Solitary Vireo *Vireo solitarius* RV
Lucy's Warbler *Vermivora luciae* AB
Yellow Warbler *Dendroica petechia* AB*
Yellow-rumped Warbler *Dendroica coronata*AV
McGillivray's Warbler *Oporornis tolmiei* RV
Summer Tanager *Piranga rubra* CB*
Western Tanager *Piranga ludoviciana* UV
Black-headed Grosbeak
  *Pheucticus melanocephalus* UV
Blue Grosbeak *Guiraca caerulea* CB*
Lazuli Bunting *Passerina amoena* RV
Green-tailed Towhee *Pipilo chlorurus* RV
Brown Towhee *Pipilo fuscus* UV
Abert's Towhee *Pipilo aberti* CB*
Chipping Sparrow *Spizella passerina* UV
Brewer's Sparrow *Spizella breweri* RV
Vesper Sparrow *Pooecetes gramineus* RV
Lark Sparrow *Chondestes grammacus* UV
Song Sparrow *Melospiza melodia* CB*
Lincoln's Sparrow *Melospiza lincolnii* RV
White-crowned Sparrow
  *Zonotrichia leucophrys* AV
Red-winged Blackbird *Agelaius phoeniceus* AV*
Western Meadowlark *Sturnella neglecta* CV
Yellow-headed Blackbird
  *Xanthocephalus xanthocephalus* RV*
Brewer's Blackbird *Euphagus cyanocephalus*UV
Great-tailed Grackle *Quiscalus mexicanus* A?*
Bronzed Cowbird *Molothrus aeneus* UB*
Brown-headed Cowbird *Molothrus ater* CB
Hooded Oriole *Icterus cucullatus* U?*
Northern Oriole *Icterus galbula* CB*
House Finch *Carpodacus mexicanus* AB
Lesser Goldfinch *Carduelis psaltria* AB*
House Sparrow *Passer domesticus* UV

although uncommon, are probably nesting. Lucy's warblers and yellow
warblers are abundant nesting birds in the orchard, as they are in native
riparian woodland (Phillips, Marshall, and Monson 1964). Blue grosbeaks,
summer tanagers, and northern orioles are common nesting birds here.
Lazuli buntings are present but uncommon, and they are probably summer visitors rather than nesters. Lesser goldfinches are abundant throughout the summer. Song sparrows, characteristically found in reed-sedge-brush
habitats along major permanent rivers (Phillips, Marshall, and Monson 1964)
are abundant in the weeds around the orchards and in slash piles and nest
in regrowth sprouts of thinned pecan trees. Abert's towhees are also present in and around the slash piles and regrowth sprouts. Red-winged blackbirds are abundant and appear to follow the irrigators, gleaning insects
flooded out of the soil by the irrigation water. I have found no nests of
these birds, but they are abundant throughout the summer, probably only
as transient foragers. Hooded orioles, common birds in native riparian woodland (Phillips, Marshall, and Monson 1964) are not common in the orchard,
and their nesting status is not known.

Some birds that might be expected in riparian habitat are apparently
absent in the orchard. The northern cardinal and Bell's vireo are apparently not present. They typically live in brushy areas along streams (Phillips, Marshall, and Monson 1964), and in the orchards there is apparently
insufficient midstory of vegetation. The vegetation profile in the orchard
is limited, offering limited diversity of foliage layers for foraging and nesting, and would effectively eliminate species that prefer the dense shrub
midstory characteristic of some native riparian woodland. Slash piles and
regrowth sprouts may be suitable for some species of midstory-frequenting
birds but not others. The slash piles are not covered by a canopy of trees,
and this may reduce their usefulness to some species. Hole-nesting birds
are rare. Woodpeckers apparently do not make holes in the pecan trees,
although three species of woodpeckers are occasionally seen in the orchard.

*Mammals.*    A number of species of mammals live in or use the orchard.
I have made no attempt to investigate the mammal fauna, except very casually. Because most species are nocturnal, casual observation has been
insufficient to get any but the most superficial understanding of the fauna.
Bats are rather abundant and appear to be of several species. They are
probably feeding on adult mosquitoes (Hinman 1934b). Coyotes, *Canis
latrans* Say, are very common, as are javelina, *Pecari tajacu* (L.). Both of
these probably eat some pecans. Raccoon *Procyon lotor* (L.) tracks and
skunk tracks are very common. Remains of road-killed striped skunks,
*Mephitis mephitis* (Schreber), are frequent along the highway running
through the orchard. Burrowing mammals appear rare or uncommon, probably because their homes would be flooded by the irrigation water. No

rodent trapping has been done in the area, so the rodent fauna is largely unknown. Cotton rats, *Sigmodon hispidus* Say and Ord, have been seen in the orchard, but their abundance and role are unknown.

## SOCIAL REPERCUSSIONS

### Economic Benefits

The farm and associated pecan shelling and packing plant employ approximately 250 people. Most of the positions are year-round, rather than seasonal, as is true in much of agriculture. Many employees are provided company-owned housing in several developments in and around the orchard. Several employees have spent most of their careers working for the farm, and there are some families with three generations working for it.

The other major industries in the area have been copper mining and real estate development. Copper mining has been very unstable and has almost completely shut down in the past three years. Real estate development is continuing to grow and provide employment, but it is, of necessity, finite and will eventually be reduced in importance as the area completes development. In the long-range development plan for the area, farming is expected to continue to be an important economic base. Pecans are a value-added specialty food product with wide distribution in the United States and Canada and a growing export market in the Pacific Rim countries. Additional important economic benefits of the farm include: interest paid on money borrowed for crop financing; custom services hired for specific purposes; equipment and chemicals purchased; support of research by several departments at the University of Arizona; and taxes paid on land, buildings, trees, payroll, equipment, vehicles, merchandise purchased, and so forth. Using standard multipliers, it is estimated that this farming enterprise has a total impact on the economy in excess of $100,000,000 per year (K. Walden, personal communication).

### Aesthetic Benefits

The community of Green Valley derived its name from the green agricultural fields that now are orchards. The pecan trees are green from April through November. The aesthetic value of this green strip which is surrounded by desert, housing developments, and closed strip mines is incalculable. In the literature, the closest comparison may be made to a study by Black et al. (1985) of the value of riparian habitat and wildlife to residents of a rapidly urbanizing community. Results of that study showed that residents value natural habitat and appreciate wildlife. Although the orchard is not native, it does provide habitat for many wildlife species. Recreational use of the orchard is limited, in that it cannot be allowed to interfere with farming operations. Hunting is not permitted and recreational vehicle use is restricted to roadways and the riverbed. Bird watchers are generally welcome. Unauthorized nut harvesting is not permitted, but is a minor problem for the growers. As development of additional housing continues in the area, some pecan trees will remain, either as individual trees among the development, or as blocks of trees in flood plain-zoned areas. The aesthetic value of mature pecans as shade trees should be high.

## Problems and Controversies

Government actions affecting agriculture have increased greatly since the orchard was planted (Walden 1984). These include regulations and policies concerning pesticide use, labor, water use, mosquito control, and burning of prunings. Government actions have generally resulted from concern for the protection of citizens or resources from real or imagined dangers. In some cases, such actions have resulted in social benefits, but in all cases they have resulted in increased costs and complications for the farmers. Because this orchard is closely associated with the retirement community of Green Valley and the small towns of Sahuarita and Continental, certain activities in the orchard concern residents.

In 1983, a newspaper reporter for the *Arizona Daily Star* learned that the farm had used Temik[R] (aldicarb) as an aphicide. Problems with aldicarb appearing in minute quantities in groundwater in Florida inspired the reporter to write a series of articles questioning whether aldicarb from the operation might contaminate the groundwater in the Santa Cruz Valley. Before the series was completed, some degree of fearful concern had been established in the community that resulted in citizen confusion and political pressure on the farm owners. Further investigation revealed that the pesticide had been used correctly and that there was little or no likelihood of aldicarb used in the orchard contaminating groundwater.

Sharply contrasting the citizens' fear of insecticide use for aphid control was the clamor for more insecticide use for mosquito control. Prior to 1983, when a program of research into mosquito control began in the area, citizen complaints to the Pima County Health Department about mosquitoes numbered from dozens to more than 100 per year. Newspapers carried prominent stories and letters to the editor from angry citizens, and considerable political pressure had developed to do something about the mosquitoes. Urban homeowners in general dislike arthropods in the urban environment (Byrne et al. 1984). Mosquitoes are especially disliked, and urban homeowners have a very low tolerance for mosquito bites (Robinson and Atkins 1983). A majority of those surveyed considered seven bites in one night as indicating a mosquito breeding problem in need of control (Robinson and Atkins 1983). The general public reaction to unwanted arthropods is to use or demand the use of chemical insecticides (Byrne and Carpenter 1983; Robinson and Atkin 1983).

The farm was blamed for all of the mosquitoes in the area, and the expense of mosquito control fell on the growers. The owners waited until citizen complaints accumulated and the Health Department directed an order to spray. Then, depending upon the severity of the problem and number of complaints, a chemical insecticide would be sprayed. This was at considerable expense: aerial spraying of the farm cost approximately $20,000 per treatment, and there might be as many as five or six treatments each year. Moreover, the effects of such spraying were only temporary on the mosquito population. In 1984, a group of citizens had organized to force the farmers to do something about the mosquitoes, with the primary stated goal being to increase insecticide spraying. As their primary weapon, this citizens' group threatened court action to enjoin the farmers from irrigating. Additional pressure had been made in the form of threats to withhold necessary zoning changes for the future development of farm property unless the mosquito problem were solved. The citizens' group and the County Health Department were persuaded to wait one month to determine if the newly started mosquito management program using *B.t.i.* would be effective. Fortunately, the new program was effective, and no complaints were made subsequent to the full-scale implementation of the plan. Both the citizens' group and the Health Department have publicly acknowledged the effectiveness of the mosquito management program, and pressure on the farmers has ceased. The growers continue, at considerable expense, to support a program of mosquito management and research. However, there are other mosquito breeding sites in areas outside the farm property that are likely to become more important now that the mosquitoes in the orchard are managed (Kingsley 1985b). It remains to be seen whether the farmers will be blamed for mosquitoes breeding off its property.

The Pima County Health Department, concerned about possible air pollution, has prohibited burning tree prunings without using a burning curtain. The required device is expensive and its use would require major redirection of labor and funds. Because prunings cannot be burned, they accumulate in large piles around the fields. These piles create excellent harborage for rock squirrels, as mentioned previously, and are a potentially serious fire hazard should they be accidentally ignited. At present, the tree prunings are selectively harvested by woodcutters for sale as firewood. Most of the wood is sold to, and burned by, area residents, thereby adding to the air pollutant load anyway.

In southern Arizona, water is a major concern. All water for municipal, industrial, and agricultural uses comes from groundwater. The water table in the Santa Cruz Valley has dropped steadily as a result of overuse, although closure of the copper mines has resulted in a slowing of the rate of decline (Hathorn 1984). The farm attempts to conserve water, within the limitations imposed by the crop requirements and their irrigation system. However, agriculture in general is repeatedly criticized for overuse of water, and recent regulations on agricultural water use complicate farm operations. Through legislation enacted in 1984, the Arizona Department of Water Resources requires metering of all wells and annual reporting of the amount of water pumped and applied to each crop. Additionally, the Tucson Active Management Area requires a water withdrawal fee of 50 cents per acre foot, which amounts to an annual tax of more than $16,000 for the farm. This water-use tax is scheduled to escalate numerous times at predetermined rates over the next several years. As part of the long-term management plan for the area, the farm owners intend to convert most of the present pecan fields to urban development, which would greatly reduce groundwater withdrawal.

## CONCLUSIONS

It is evident that a land-use decision based upon economic considerations has resulted in the creation of an agricultural ecosystem that has profound biological and social repercussions. New wildlife habitat, closely resembling important but declining native habitat, has been created and settled by native animals. The development of the habitat and management of the farm have had important repercussions for the local economy, politics, and environment. Long-term plans will result in many changes in this dynamic system.

## ACKNOWLEDGMENTS

This research was supported by grants from Farmers' Investment Company and Zoecon Corporation. Grateful acknowledgment is due the following reviewers of the manuscript: Keith Walden, R. R. Johnson, and the Department of Entomology Manuscript Review Committee consisting of F. G. Werner, W. L. Nutting, and D. N. Byrne, two anonymous reviewers, and the editor of this volume, J. O. Schmidt.

# REFERENCES

Bach, D., Kuykendall, J. R. 1971. Trickle irrigation for pecan orchards. *Pecan Quart.* 5(2): 11–15.

Black, S., Broadhurst, P., Hightower, J., Schauman, S. 1985. The value of riparian habitat and wildlife to the residents of a rapidly urbanizing community. See Johnson et al. (1985), 410–15.

Brison, F. R. 1974. *Pecan Culture.* Austin, TX: Capital Print. 294 pp.

Byrne, D. N., Carpenter, E. H. 1983. Behavior of metropolitan and non-metropolitan residents relative to urban pest control strategies. *Southwest. Entomol.* 8:198–204.

Byrne, D. N., Carpenter, E. H., Thoms, E. M., Cotty, S. T. 1984. Public attitudes toward urban arthropods. *Bull. Entomol. Soc. Am.* 30(2): 40–44.

Conine, K. H., Anderson, B. W., Ohmart, R. D., Drake, J. F. 1978. Responses of riparian species to agricultural habitat conversions. *See* Johnson and McCormick (1978), 248–62.

Corbet, P. S. 1980. Biology of Odonata. *Ann. Rev. Entomol.* 25:189–217.

Couch, G. A. 1981. Wildlife control in pecans. *Proc. Texas Pecan Growers Assoc.* 60:52–55.

Gaines, D. 1977. The valley riparian forests of California: their importance to bird populations. *See* Sands (1977), 57–85.

Harris, M. K. 1983. Integrated pest management of pecans. *Ann. Rev. Entomol.* 28:291–318.

Hathorn, S., Jr. 1984. 1984 Arizona Pecan Budgets: Pima/Pinal Counties. Tucson: Dept. of Agri. Econ. Univ. of Ariz. 92 pp.

Hinman, E. H. 1934a. Predators of the Culicidae (mosquitoes). I. The predators of larvae and pupae, exclusive of fish. *J. Trop. Med. Hyg.* 37:(9): 129–34.

———. 1934b. Predators of the Culicidae (mosquitoes). II. Predators of adult mosquitoes. *J. Trop. Med. Hyg.* 37(10): 145–50.

James, H. G. 1964. The role of Coleoptera in the natural control of mosquitos in Canada. *Proc. Intern. Congr. Entomol.* 12:357–58.

Johnson, R. R., Carothers, S. W. 1982. Riparian habitat and recreation: interrelationships and impacts in the Southwest and Rocky Mountain region. Eisenhower Consortium Bulletin 12, Rocky Mt. For. and Range Exp. Stn., USDA For. Serv., Fort Collins, CO. 31 pp.

Johnson, R. R., Jones, D. A., tech. coords. 1977. Importance, preservation and management of riparian habitat: a symposium. (Tucson, AZ, 9 July 1977). USDA For. Serv. Tech. Rep. RM-43, Rocky Mt. For. and Range Exp. Stn., Fort Collins, CO. 217 pp.

Johnson, R. R., McCormick, J. F., tech. coords. 1978. Strategies for protection and management of floodplain wetlands and other riparian ecosystems. (Proc. symp., Callaway Gardens, GA., Dec. 11-13, 1978.) USDA For. Serv. Gen. Tech. Rep. WO-12, USDA For. Serv., Wash., D.C. 410 pp.

Johnson, R. R., Ziebell, C. D., Patton, D. R., Ffolliott, P. F., Hamre, R. H., tech. coords. 1985. Riparian ecosystems and their management: reconciling conflicting uses. First North American Riparian Conference, April 16-18, 1985, Tucson, AZ. Gen. Tech. Rep. RM-120. USDA For. Serv. Rocky Mt. For. and Range Exp. Stn., Fort Collins, CO. 523 pp.

Jones, K. B., Glinski, P. C. 1985. Microhabitats of lizards in a southwestern riparian community. *See* Johnson et al. (1985), 342–46.

Kingsley, K. J. 1985a. The pecan orchard as a riparian ecosystem. *See* Johnson et al. (1985), 245–49.

———. 1985b. Bionomics and management of pest mosquitoes at the agro-urban interface Santa Cruz Valley, Arizona. Ph.D. dissertation. Univ. of Arizona, Tucson. 143 pp.

Legner, E. G., Sjogren, R. D. 1984. Biological mosquito control furthered by advances in technology and research. *Mosquito News* 44:449–56.

Leser, J. F. 1981. Effects of temperature and host-insect interaction on the population dynamics of the blackmargined aphid, *Monellia caryella* (Fitch) (Homoptera: Aphididae). Ph.D. dissertation. Univ. of Arizona, Tucson. 128 pp.

Lowe, C. H. 1985. Amphibians and reptiles in southwest riparian ecosystem. *See* Johnson et al. (1985), 339–41.

Margalit, J., Dean, D. 1985. The story of *Bacillus thuringiensis* var. *israelensis (B.t.i.)*. *J. Am. Mosq. Control Assoc.* 1:1–7.

Martin, A. C., Zim, H. S., Nelson, A. L. 1951. *American Wildlife and Plants.* New York: Dover. 500 pp.

McLaughlin, R. E., Vidrine, M. F. 1984. Distribution of *Bacillus thuringiensis* (H-14) by water during flooding of rice fields. *Mosquito News* 44:36–42.

Mielke, E. A., True, L. F. 1981. *Pecans in Arizona.* Tucson: Cooperative Extension Service, University of Arizona. 12 pp.

Miller, E., Miller D. R. 1980. Snag use by birds. In *Workshop Proceedings: Management of Western Forests and Grasslands for Nongame Birds* (Feb. 11-14, 1980, Salt Lake City, Utah). Comp. R. M. DeGraaf, N. G. Tilghman, 337–56. USDA For. Serv. Gen. Tech. Rep. INT-86, Intermt. For. and Range Exp. Stn., Ogden, UT. 535 pp.

Miura, T., Takahashi, R. M., Mulligan, F. S., III, 1978. Field evaluation of the effectiveness of predacious insects as a mosquito control agent. *Proc. Calif. Mosquito Control Assoc.* 46:80–81.

Monson, G., Phillips, A. R. 1981. *Annotated checklist of the birds of Arizona.* 2d ed. Tucson: University of Arizona Press. 240 pp.

Mullenax, R. H., Polles, S. G., Gibson, P. 1984. Squirrel damage and squirrel control in pecan orchards. *Pecan South* 11(1):22–23.

Mulligan, F. S., III, Schaefer, C. H. 1981. Integration of a selective mosquito control agent *Bacillus thuringiensis* serotype H-14 with natural predator populations in pesticide-sensitive habitats. *Proc. Calif. Mosquito Control Assoc.* 49:30–35.

Ohmart, R. D., Anderson, B. W., Hunter, W. C. 1985. Influence of agriculture on waterbird, wader, and shorebird use along the lower Colorado River. *See* Johnson et al. (1985), 117–22.

Olkowski, W., Daar, S. 1985. Update: plague on the rise. *IPM Practitioner* 7(10):1–8.

Phillips, A., Marshall, J., Monson, G. 1964. *The Birds of Arizona.* Tucson: University of Arizona Press. 212 pp.

Robinson, W. H., Atkins, R. L. 1983. Attitudes and knowledge of urban homeowners towards mosquitoes. *Mosquito News* 43:38–41.

Sands, A., ed. 1977. *Riparian Forests in California, Their Ecology and Conservation.* Berkeley: Div. of Agri. Sciences, Univ. of Calif. Priced Pub. 4101. 122 pp.

Walden, R. K. 1970. Why and how to establish a pecan orchard in the West. *Proc. Texas Pecan Growers Assoc.* 49:43–47.

Walden, R. S. 1984. The sunset and the new dawn. *18th West. Pecan Conf. Proc.* 137–40.

Warner, R. E., Hendrix, K. M., eds. 1984. California riparian systems: ecology, conservation, and productive management. (Based on proc. of conf. at Davis, Calif., 17–19 Sept. 1981.) Berkeley: University of California Press. 1035 pp.

Warren, P. L., Schwalbe, C. R. 1985. Herpetofauna in riparian habitats along the Colorado River in Grand Canyon. *See* Johnson et al. (1985), 347–54.

Wells, D., Anderson, B. W., Ohmart, R. D. 1979. Comparative avian use of Southwestern citrus orchard and riparian communities. *J. Ariz.-Nev. Acad. Sci.* 14:53–58.

Wolstenholme, B. N. 1979. The ecology of pecan trees, part 1: characteristics of the native habitat. *Pecan Quart.* 13(2): 32–35.

Zalom, F. G., Grigarick, A. A. 1980. Predation by *Hydrophilus triangularis* and *Tropisternus lateralis* in California rice fields. *Ann. Entomol. Soc. Amer.* 73:167–71.

# CONTRIBUTORS

James C. Fogleman
Department of Biological Sciences
University of Denver
Denver, Colorado

William B. Heed
Department of Ecology and Evolutionary Biology
University of Arizona
Tucson, Arizona

Susan C. Jones
Forest Service, U.S. Department of Agriculture
Southern Forest Experiment Station
Gulfport, Mississippi

Kenneth J. Kingsley
Department of Entomology
University of Arizona
Tucson, Arizona

William P. MacKay
Department of Biology
New Mexico State University
Las Cruces, New Mexico

William L. Nutting
Department of Entomology
University of Arizona
Tucson, Arizona

Justin O. Schmidt
Southwestern Biological Institute
Tucson, Arizona

Patricia J. Schmidt
Department of Entomology
University of Arizona
Tucson, Arizona
Southwestern Biological Institute
Tucson, Arizona

152

Walter G. Whitford
Department of Biology
New Mexico State University
Las Cruces, New Mexico

John C. Zak
Department of Biology
New Mexico State University
Las Cruces, New Mexico